HEARD ON THE PLAYGROUND

Funny Things Kids Say

Andrea Sherr

HUGO HOUSE PUBLISHERS, LTD.

ISBN: 978-1-936449-15-6 (Paperback)

Library of Congress Control Number: 2011936446

Cover Design and Interior Layout: Ronda Taylor, www.taylorbydesign.com

Cover Illustration: Valerie Sherr

Published by:

Hugo House Publishers, Ltd.
Englewood, CO
Austin, TX
(877) 700-0616
www.HugoHousePublishers.com

About the Illustrators

Valarie has been studying art for seven years which is a long time considering she is only eight. She is self-taught having started off using crayons and has worked into more advanced mediums like markers, colored pencils and pastels. The world is her canvas as is evidenced by the fact that her work can often be found on her t-shirts, her walls and her little brother's belly and bum. Valarie hopes to one day exhibit her art (minus her brother's rear) in a real art gallery in between being a legendary horseback rider, hip hop superstar, and concert pianist.

Zoë was born wanting to draw. At five years old, she is already a prolific artist. While most of her creations have been washed down the drain—her legs are still her favorite canvas—she has filled one large storage container with her art—and that was only from one year of preschool. While crayons are not her favorite medium (she much prefers markers and water colors to express her artistic vision), she obliged her mother, the publisher, to draw various doo-dads and pictures of whatever her mother requested. She is very excited to have her art exhibited in a real book. It's giving her ideas for her own edition.

Rosie is not only a friend to Valarie and her older brother, she is also a contributing illustrator. Rosie was hand selected to illustrate this book based on her artistic ability, friendship status, and close proximity to our house (she lives five doors down). Only ten years old, Rosie is multi-talented and accomplished having mastered the art of drawing, cooking and mediating fights between Val and her older brother. She is the only person we know who can keep Val's older brother in line.

The students at the Detroit Country Day lower school in Mrs. Park's class were all such talented artists; it made it hard to choose which of their drawings to include in this book. I wanted to include them all, but that almost gave my editor a heart attack. It was a privilege to work with these students.

Mitchel and Spencer (the brothers) didn't contribute any artwork for reasons I won't mention though I will hint at—one only draws things that can be destroyed or blown up and the other doesn't even know his alphabet yet. However, I must say they did offer support often in the form of...when your book does well can you buy me something? Also, since Val is mentioned here, there'd be big trouble if they weren't mentioned as well.

Dedication

This book is for all the hard working Moms, Dads, Grandparents, Teachers and Child Caregivers...you all deserve a good laugh.

For my business-minded husband who supported me, even without seeing a business plan. (See? You do love me!)

To my entertaining children who provided me with the idea and material for this book (even if they didn't exactly provide me with the time). And a special thank you to my daughter, Valarie, who helped to illustrate the book with her drawings whenever she could fit me into her busy 7-year-old schedule.

And to my mom who never runs out of advice and has shown me the true meaning of unconditional love.

Contents

Introduction

You don't know me, but you've seen me or you may even be like me (though you'd never admit it publicly). I'm that Mom. You know the one at the Mall attracting all the unwanted attention as I desperately try to control my "fun loving kids"; I'm that Mom who drives in my nightgown at 11 pm to pick up a casualty from a sleep over that went awry; I'm that Mom who's so busy I forget to look in the mirror and walk around with messy hair and disheveled clothes; I'm that Mom who, when trying to teach her child a lesson in public, was asked by complete strangers to please just give the kid anything he wants. I'm that Mom I always thought I'd never be...before I had kids.

But you know what, I've discovered once you let go of those dreams of perfect children who immediately obey your every command and harmoniously play together like the Cleaver's and the Brady's. Yeah once I let go of those delusions of a picture-perfect family, I actually found it was more fun on the other side. The other side, for those who are unfamiliar, is where you learn to laugh at things that you once believed to be sacred and fundamental about life.

These are the basic "Things" like the right not to discuss pooping and peeing; The right to enjoy a meal without discussing in depth how the animal on your plate was slaughtered; The right to age gracefully while not being reminded everyday how ancient you are (not having had cell phones growing up) and how many body parts are becoming wrinkly and turning grey. These are the conversations that replace the mundane and civilized exchanges at the dinner table like "Pass the peas" or "How was your day?"

With this unexpected life, my three children provide more than enough opportunity to see the humor in life, which is a nice way of saying it's better to laugh than face the reality that I've lost total control, and should abandon my children to devote myself to the study of parenting manuals like the Ferber Method and Parenting with Love and Logic.

I mean isn't it better to laugh when trying to reason with my screaming three year old for the hundredth time as to why I can't sit in backseat with him while driving. Why deny someone like me a little humor as I ask my older son to continue to keep his hidden talent hidden by not telling anyone else his penie can talk. And why not let me smile politely at the three security guards, four TSA agents and countless passengers who assist me in getting my seven year old on a plane. Come on people, humor is the only thing at these moments that keeps me from doing a reenactment of *The Shining* or *One Flew Over the Cuckoo's Nest.*

Sure, I've seriously considered throwing in the "Mommy towel" to pursue a career taming wild animals since I clearly have the qualifications. However, I feel l have a moral obligation not to burden society. So instead I hang in there.

Clearly no one would have faulted me for trying to develop multiple personalities, seeking asylum in Siberia or even offering my children up to the Pentagon to interrogate prisoners (forget water boarding...just force the prisoners to babysit my three for a few hours and they'll be talking in no time). Though these options are definitely appealing, I decided to take a different path.

Just like E.T. I knew there had to be others out there like me, so I started slowly by whispering to Moms in the school hallways asking for their funny kid stories. To my surprise and relief, there were lots of Moms looking to share the embarrassing, hysterical, and shocking things their kids had said and done. Suddenly I was emboldened to reach out to more people. Rapidly teachers, grandparents, friends, relatives and babysitters were contacting me with laughable moments they had been waiting to share.

I quickly realized it would be almost criminal not to share all these hilarious stories that had no place to go for the last twenty five years since the 1980's when *Kids Say the Darndest Things* was cancelled. So I started, HeardonthePlayground.com, a website where everyone contributes and shares their funny kid stories. Like all my ideas, they sound easier on paper than in practice.

Developing and running HeardonthePlayground.com has resulted in many unexpected challenges, none of which any typical CEO has ever had to face. I've had to deal with kids screaming in the background during business calls; taking notes during a conference call with a purple crayon while sitting at a water park; surviving a two year old using my body as a jungle gym during meetings; withstanding emotional blackmail from my nine year old who asked if I "loved the computer more than him?" And waking up at three a.m. to a husband asking what my revenue model is. The normal office politics and stress pale in comparison to what I've had to face launching a website and publishing a book.

I did get a stroke of luck with the book publication, though. I had to keep costs down since I'm sleeping with my investor who also happens to be my husband (note to all never sleep with your investor). So I desperately looked for a talented illustrator who was readily available and dirt cheap. After ruling out my ten year old due to his lack of commitment to anything that doesn't involving a ball or a stick, and disqualifying my three year old due to his limited artistic repertoire of four shapes and three colors, I settled upon my seven year old daughter as the most qualified candidate to illustrate this book.

After serious negotiations that will remain confidential (though I can mention Toys-R-Us and trips to water parks were involved) we hammered out an acceptable deal. I'm thrilled my seven year old was available to illustrate my book and could fit me into her hectic schedule between American Girl Doll Camp, the Hungry Planet Video games and feeding her fish.

In the end, though, all the hard work has been worth it. With every new and hysterical kid story I receive, I'm assured that the sanity and peace I've lost is worth the laughter and joy I've gained. I hope you enjoy this book as much as I have enjoyed creating it.

My five-year-old daughter was watching me as I applied a green facial mask. Curious she asked "What are you doing Mommy?" I replied "I'm putting a mask on my face to make me look prettier." Five minutes later my daughter followed me into the bathroom as I removed the mask with a wet cotton ball. Concerned she said, "Mommy, did you give up?"

Anonymous, 5 – Kansas

My daughter accidently saw her daddy taking a shower, and I didn't think it had much of an effect on her until bedtime when she said her prayers. That night's prayers went something like this, "I want to pray for Daddy because he's sick. I discovered he has a tail like a doggy. God please heal him."

Linda, 5 – Massachusetts

While reviewing colors with my daughter she confessed, "Mom, sometimes I forget what gray is, then I remember it's the color I see when you lift up your bangs."

MacKenzie, 6 – Utah
Jonbonjovious.blogspot.com

When my granddaughter, Lily, was three years old, she and her mom went to visit Grandpa in San Diego. While there, they attended church. After the service Lily's Grandpa introduced them to an interracial couple with a young baby. Lily's Mom said, "Look how beautiful she is Lily. You used to be just like that." Lily blurted out, "I used to be black?"

Lily, 3 – Maine

My hair is getting too gray for my taste. Wanting a change in hair color, I told my husband I was going to the "dark side." My son, Noah, is a huge Star Wars fan and immediately started tearing up. In desperation he cried, "No Mommy, please don't do it. Don't go to the dark side like Darth Vader."

Noah, 6 – South Carolina

My husband and son were boasting about their abs. My husband said "Look Evan we both have six packs." Without missing a beat, my son replied, "Yeah, but yours are in the cooler."

Evan, 9 – Michigan

My son is facinated with heavy construction equipment. I thought this was a harmless interest until we were at the supermarket one day behind a rather large woman. When her cell phone rang my son suddenly shouted excitedly "Watch out Mom she's backing up!"

Daniel, 6 – Illinois

My daughter got into my makeup, so I hid it. About an hour later, she came out of her bedroom to tell me, "I don't need your makeup anymore, I have my own." I immediately understood what she meant since it was written all over her face in permanent marker as eye shadow, blush, and lipstick.

Lucy, 5 – Mississippi

I took my seven year old to the doctor for a physical and shots. At the end of the examination, the nurse, who happened to be rather abrupt, walked in with the needle and asked, "Which arm would you like your shot in?" In a harsh voice my daughter looked her straight in the eye and replied, "Yours."

Anonymous, 7 – Massachusetts

I have small breasts, which I was fine with until one day when my son said "Oh, Mommy, I see your boobies. Are you okay with how big they are? I mean, do you wish they were real big like Daddy's?"

Tanner, 3 – California

One day my two-year-old daughter, Jennifer, was playing in the backyard with her friend, Karen. When they came running into the house, I noticed Karen had switched her shoes around so the left was on the right foot and vice versa. "Karen honey, your shoes are on the wrong feet," I told her. She stopped, looked down at her feet then up at me with a confused expression and said, "But these are the only feet I got."

Karen, 2 – Nebraska

My mother took my son, Leo, to get a haircut. Leo was not happy as they clipped his curls off and was on the verge of crying. When the barber was done his Grandma smiled and said "You look like a little man now." Horrified my son cried, "Give me back my hair. I want to look like a little boy again."

Leo, 5 – Ohio

It was bath time and I told my son he had to wash his hair (the number one thing he hates doing). I noticed his hair was getting long and mentioned he'd need a haircut (his second most hated thing). With a look of disgust he replied, "Then maybe we shouldn't water it so much."

Matthew – West Virginia

Being a nanny is the best job on earth, especially when you have a very observant child to look after. One morning, I came to work broken out in pimples and felt extremely self-conscious. Sophie, a smiley two year old, immediately greeted me with a hug making which made me feel much better until she added "Why do you have so many nipples on your cheek?"

Sophie, 2 – Arizona

After putting up with Ella's bad behavior the entire day, I told my daughter I knew everything she did because I had eyes in the back of my head. After Dad arrived home, Ella met him at the door with the exciting news that Mommy had four eyes.

Ella, 4 – Ohio

My two daughters, three and five years old, were jumping on the bed. I was trying to discourage them from doing this and said, "Girls you're going to knock the snot out of your noses if you keep jumping like that." My three year old promptly asked, "What is snot?" And my five year old confidently answered, "It's Spanish for boogers."

Anonymous, 5 – Vermont

Trying to teach my son a valuable lesson I told him, "Your friend, David, shoved a crayon in his ear and had to go to the hospital to have it removed by a doctor. I hope you learn a lesson from that." I thought I got my point across until my son asked, "What color was the crayon?"

Nick, 5 – New Mexico

My friend's cat recently gave birth to a litter of kittens. I took my kids over to see the little darlings. When my son observed his siblings gently stroking the kitties he yelled, "Mom, I want to pet the titties too."

Corey, 6 – Michigan

When Kael was three, he was asked by a teacher at snack time, "Would you like seconds on the cookies?" "No," he replied, "if I have seconds I will blow up like a fat ball. I know it can happen because it happened to my mom."

Kael, 3 – Kentucky

While sitting around the dinner table, my daughter noticed the centerpiece of wildflowers I'd put together after our walk outside. The beautiful flowers poked out of the vase going in all directions. My daughter took one look at the centerpiece and said "Mom the flowers look just like you." I was so touched by her sweet remark until she added, "because you're having a bad hair day."

Lani, 5 – Michigan

My sister told my son, "If you keep eating too much candy, your teeth are going to fall out." Not fazed at all, my son replied, "Who cares...I'm getting a new set anyways."

Anonymous, 5 – North Carolina

When my daughter was four, she asked "Mommy when will I get a booby trap?" I looked at her, confused, and asked "What do you mean honey?" She touched her chest and said, "You know, a booby trap... for my boobies." I couldn't help but laugh at her fairly accurate description of a bra.

Anonymous, 4 – Montana

My four-year-old daughter was watching TV when a commercial for Lactaid came on advertising its benefits for those who were lactose intolerant. At the end of the ad, my daughter came up to me and announced that she too was "black toast intolerant."

Anonymous, 4 – New York

FAMILY

My kids were being particularly rowdy while playing. Worried someone was going to get hurt, I yelled at my son, "Stop climbing on your sister or you'll get a time out." Without pausing, my son shot back at me, "You're not the boss of me...Mom is."

Dave, 5 – Mississippi

As a Mom who works outside the home, I look forward to the occasional week day I have off with the boys. However, at home all I hear is "Mom, get me some milk," '"Mom can I have something to eat," and "Mom can we make cookies?" It was exhausting. Finally, I had enough and told the kids "Being home and waiting on you guys makes me feel like a lousy maid." My littlest guy hugged my leg and comforted me by saying, "No Mom, you're a really good maid."

Anonymous, 8 – New York

A couple years ago I took my son, Joe, fishing. It was a group fishing expedition that included people who were obviously hearing impaired and using sign language. We sat without catching any fish while the hearing impaired group caught one fish after the other. Frustrated, my son left to use the bathroom on the boat. When he returned, I noticed he had wads of paper stuck in both ears.

Joe, 8 – Maine

My daughter and my son were fighting one day when my son came to me and said that my daughter had scratched him really hard. I asked her if that was true. So she looked at me with the most innocent face ever and said, "I didn't scratch him, his arm walked into my nail."

Hattie, 6 – Tennessee

After hearing the story of the three little pigs and the big bad wolf, my three-year-old son asked, "Why didn't they just call the Wonder Pets for help?"

Rory, 3 – Georgia

My older daughter and her friends were playing with Barbies pretending they had careers which led to a conversation about what they were going to be when they grew up. Shaina, my youngest, chimed in, "I'm going to be a mermaid and live in the sea." One of the older girls said, "You can't, there are no such things as mermaids." Unfazed, Shaina replied, "Then I'll be the first one."

Shaina, 5 – Ohio

I was quizzing my daughter on animal sounds the other day. I asked her "What does a kitty say?" She responded "Meow." Next I asked, "What does a doggy say?" She replied "Woof." Lastly I tried to trick her by asking "And what does a deer say?" She exclaimed "Pow, Pow!"

Dakota, 2 – Iowa

When my daughter was misbehaving, my husband warned, "Stop acting up, you know Santa's watching you." Our five year old looked him straight in the eye and said, "No he's not, Santa is at the mall."

Jordan, 5 – Tennessee

I was leaving Grandma's house when four large deer ran in front of my car. As my life flashed before my eyes, I hear my little princess saying in awe "Were those Santa's reindeers?"

Anonymous, 6 – West Virginia

Upon hearing me say, "I'm claustrophobic" my daughter gasped and said, "Mom, you mean you're afraid of Santa Claus?"

Isabella, 7 – California

As I waited in line with my son to see Santa at the mall, he looked perplexed and said to me "Dad, Santa is so skinny. Did he borrow Mom's South Beach diet book? Amused I replied, "Maybe." My son added, "Well, I guess I'll tell Mommy to leave him turkey lettuce wraps instead of cookies this year."

Derek, 7 – Minnesota

My daughter had to choose a person (dead or alive) whom she would most like to meet as the subject of her school essay. Coming from a liberal, democratic household her natural choice was none other than...Sarah Palin. She's not even a teenager and the rebellion has already begun.

Molly, 10 – Michigan

We took our two older kids on a trip to New York City and left our three year old behind with Grandma. We were gone two days when he became very sad telling his Grandma, "Mommy and Daddy left on a plane...and they forgot me."

Spencer, 3 – Michigan

After many visits to the time out chair, my daughter still refused to listen. Finally, I grounded her (for the first time). Pouting and sticking her lower lip out, she asked, "How long do I have be on the ground?"

Gretchen, 2 – Ohio

I picked my two kids up from school, only to discover my oldest had been playing in the dirt. So I asked him to wash his hands. "Mama, you just tell me what to do and I'll do it" he replied. I was so impressed that I stopped a random teacher in the hallway and told her what he said. She thought I was talking about my younger child and said in disbelief "He said that?" I corrected her, "No, his older brother said that." Not wanting to be out done, my younger child interjected, "Mama, you just tell me what to do, and I'll do the opposite."

Anonymous, 5 – California
Yeahgoodtimes.blogspot.com

We were moving to a state on the other side of the country, so I told my wife we should both drive a car. Hearing this, our son, Nathan, looked worried and said, "How will we keep from getting separated?" I reassured him, "We'll drive slowly so one car can follow the other." Still not convinced he said "Yeah, but what if we do get separated?" Teasing him a bit I replied, "Well then I guess we'll never see each other again." Without hesitation he told me "Okay, then I'm riding with Mom."

Nathan, 8 – Pennsylvania

Upset that my son kept asking for things, I told him "You need to earn extra money to buy the toys you want." I expected him to negotiate with me for an allowance and was surprised when he said, "Fine, I'm going to sell my sister on e-bay." I actually considered this a positive sign since just the other day he tried to give his sister away.

Martin, 8 – Maine

Waiting for the Fourth of July fireworks to start, my daughter invited herself into a nearby tent where a number of kids had gathered. We taught her it was polite to introduce herself to new people, so she went right up to the group of kids and said "My name is Lani Catherine Parks Tinkerbell Cinderella...I come from a long line of princesses."

Lani, 5 – Michigan

Siblings Aiden and Lily were arguing (for a change!)

Daddy," Aiden asks, "Is trash a bad word?"

"Why, no, Aiden." Dad replies. "Trash is just another word for garbage."

"Good," says Aiden and turns to his sister.

"Lily, You're trash."

Aiden, 4-New Jersey

"Love will find you even if you're trying to hide from it. I've been trying to hide from it since I was five, but the girls keep finding me."

Dave, 8 - Illinois

My niece and nephew were fighting about whom their Mom liked most. Danny said, "I am the youngest, and everyone always likes the baby the most. "That's not true," said Molly, suggesting they let Liza their older sister vote. "She doesn't like either of you best because it's me she likes most" said Liza. "How do you know?" asked Danny. "Because she met me first and has known me the longest" Liza replied confidently.

Liza, 9 Arizona

My brother lives out of state, so we hadn't seen him in years when he decided to come for a visit. I was busy when the doorbell rang, and I told my daughter to answer it. Not remembering her uncle, my daughter ran back to tell me "A big, tall, bald man dressed in a white shirt and pants with an earring is at the door. He says he's Uncle Phil, but I'm pretty sure it's Mr. Clean."

Gretchen, 7 – Ohio

My thirteen-year-old son is intelligent beyond his years. One day he casually looked at me and said "Mom, you should be cryogenically frozen." I said "Now?" "No, when you're done raising me" he replied. "What is it I do to raise you? You don't listen to anything I say," I informed him. My son answered, "You pay for everything and because of that I take into consideration what you say."

Anonymous, 13 – New York

This is a recent conversation I overheard between my son and daughter. "Why were you the first born?" my daughter asked. "Because God wanted a boy first in our family then a girl, girl and another girl," my son responded. "Well that's not right...it's always supposed be ladies first" my daughter protested.

Caidee, 5 – California
Thetrendytreehouse.blogspot.com

My daughter recently informed me "Mommy, when I prayed to God for you to have two babies, I didn't mean two bad babies."

Izzy, 7 – Tennessee

My seven and nine year olds were arguing at the kitchen table as I prepared dinner. Tired of the bickering I said, "I'd like to see more conversation." Mitch looked confused for a moment and then smiled and said "Val you're an idiot." Shocked I yelled, "Why did you just say that?" Mitch replied "You said you wanted more confrontation so I'm doing what you said." What a difference a few letters make.

Mitch, 9 – Oregon

Eythen recently told me that he doesn't have to pick up his room. Why you might ask? Well according to my son "Isn't that what Moms do? Dads build things and fix toilets. Moms clean and shop." I want to extend an apology to Eythen's future wife right now.

Eythen, 5 – Kansas

I was in a hurry and became ever more frustrated at hitting all the red lights. My daughter who was in the backseat had a very different perspective as she commented, "Mommy you're so lucky you get to be line leader."

Kate, 6 – Massachusetts

Mom, when I'm grown up and have a wife, we're going to have Happy Meals for lunch every day that way we can stay happy and married forever.

Nick, 6 – Colorado
Peelinganorangewithascrewdriver.blogspot.com

I got the flu so my thoughtful (and opportunistic) son, Eythen, asked if he could stay home from school to take care of me. I thought it was such a heart-warming gesture until he added "Is it okay if I play with my Wii and trains all day unless you need something really important like Sprite?"

Eythen, 6 – Kansas
Moorepartyof5.blogspot.com

"Why didn't you clean the bathroom like I asked?" I said to my daughter. "It was too dirty" she replied.

Anonymous, 9 – Arizona

My young daughter and I were driving past a factory, where tall smokestacks blew out puffy, billows of smoke. My daughter took one look at the scene and commented excitedly, "Look, Mom, that's how clouds are really made."

Anonymous, 6 – Ohio

It had been a long day, and it was finally time to read a bedtime story to my little boy. I was tired, and admittedly I "skimmed" over some parts of the book thinking he wouldn't notice. About halfway through, my son interrupted me and said "You know Mommy, the story makes much more sense when you read all of the parts."

Dylan, 4 – Georgia
Princessmuffintop.blogspot.com

My daughter's friend, Alyssa, had parents that were divorced. Alyssa told Gretchen how she got two allowances, two Christmases and two birthdays. Gretchen listened intently then returned home later that day and said, "Mommy, any chance you and Daddy might get a divorce?"

Gretchen, 5 – Ohio

I was having a conversation about changing my last name after my upcoming wedding when I asked my three year old, Rowan "Do you know what your full name is?" Without hesitating she replied "Sure, it's Rowan Devine Come Here Right Now."

Rowan, 3 – Florida

My three-year-old son exclaimed, "Look princess dresses, I want to be a princess." I informed him "Boys aren't supposed to be princesses." He seemed a little perplexed and then replied, "Okay then I'll be a queen."

LP, 3 – New Hampshire

"What do you want to be when you grow up?" I asked my son. "A superhero who can shoot laser beams from my eyes" he replied without hesitating. Then my son looked at me with a serious face and asked, "And what do you want to be when you grow up Dad? The same thing?"

Anonymous, 8 – Ohio

I was cleaning the kitchen when my son yelled from the family room, "Mommy, come look at my lego tower." "I'll be there in a minute," I responded. After a moment's pause, my son hollered back, "Is that going to be a real minute or a Mommy minute?"

Anonymous, 5 —Alaska

REAL MINUTE   MOMMY MINUTE

My daughter was mouthing off and trying to distract me (in every way she could think of) from making dinner. Finally, I said, "Gracie, you're getting on my last nerve." She immediately shot right back, "You're getting on all of my nerves."

Gracie, 5 – Louisiana

I was a single mom and naturally, money was tight. One day I stopped at a red light across the street from Kentucky Fried Chicken, my three-year-old daughter's favorite place. She got all excited and asked if we could get some 'tucky chicken. When I told her "No" she asked "Why Not?" I answered truthfully telling her "I need to pay bills first and then we can see about getting chicken." Looking confused she asked, "Who is Bill and why are you always paying him?"

Anonymous, 3 – Washington

Makenzie and her mom were talking about what they were going to get Dad for Father's Day. Makenzie's cousin heard the conversation and commented that he didn't know where his daddy lives. Makenzie immediately said, "You can borrow my daddy if you want."

Makenzie, 3 – Colorado

My daughter came to me filled with excitement and said "Look Mommy, I found a whole bunch of princess dresses in your top drawer." Unfortunately she had discovered my sheer negligees.

Addie, 3 – New Jersey

Back when my daughter was three years old, and I still walked on water, she asked "Dad, how much is twenty?" I answered, "Well, it's one plus nineteen, or it's two plus eighteen, or it's three plus seventeen." Shocked she replied, "You mean you don't know?"

Emily, 3 – Oklahoma

We were moving into a new neighborhood with lots of young families. I left to get cleaning supplies and upon returning found my daughter squatting in the front yard trying to poop like Murphy, our dog, while my husband stood on a ladder oblivious. To make matters worse, at that very moment a new neighbor walked by with her well behaved baby and dog.

Anonymous, 2 – South Carolina

My son kept nagging me during the day so I finally turned to him and said, "You're driving me crazy." He looked me straight in the eye and replied, "That's impossible, I can't even drive yet."

Mac, 3 – Washington

At dinner last night, the waitress asked my son "May I take your drink order?" He said, "I want a strawberry milkshake." The waitress then said "Mom, is that okay?" Astounded, my son asked, "How did you know my mom's name?"

Anonymous, 6 – Kentucky

My daughter nonchalantly informed me of her aspirations in life saying, "I want to be a weather floor crapper when I grow up." I'm hoping she meant a weather forecaster.

Rebecca, 6 – North Carolina

The kids and I were in the van following behind my husband's car. My husband turned off the exit, and we continued on the highway. Abruptly my daughter asked, "Where is Daddy's head going?" (Where is Daddy headed?)

Sellee, 3 – Ohio
Pays2save.com

While discussing boys, my daughter observed, "Dates are for having fun and getting to know each other...even boys have something to say if you listen long enough."

Lynnette, 8 – Florida

My daughter was a first year ballet student, which meant lots of ballet recitals. One time we brought all three boys to watch her performance. Our eldest son has a tremendous phobia of all things feminine. At some point, the pink tutus and tights became more than my son could take so he blurted out, "I'm in hell". I reached around to give him one of those parental pinches when he said in a rather poetic manner fitting the angst of an eight-year-old boy "The knife of the spirit of embarrassment has slit my throat."

Silas, 8 – North Carolina

When getting out of the car, my son always demands "Mom unplug me now!" (Unbuckle)

Reed, 3 – Michigan

My son was dirty and didn't want to take a shower so he threatened, "You'd better let me take a shower tomorrow or else." Cautiously I asked "Or else what?" In a defiant voice my son replied "Or else something so evil will happen I haven't even thought of it yet!

Dominick, 5 – Iowa

On a bus, my daughter took a chocolate bar from my purse, and I jokingly asked her who took it. She immediately turned to the man sitting nearby (whom we didn't know) and said with conviction, "He did it."

Anonymous, 3 – New York

"Close the curtains," requested our two-year-old granddaughter, sitting in a pool of bright light. "The sun's looking at me too hard."

Caroline, 2 – South Carolina

"If you gave me something special, what would it be?" my son asked out of the blue one day. Thinking of all the wonderful things I could give him I decided upon "Health, happiness and a good life." Looking a bit unsatisfied my son replied, "I was thinking more along the lines of a cell phone or flat screen TV."

George, 7 – Alabama

I hired a baby nurse for a few weeks after the birth of my twins. This allowed me to ease my older daughter , Sara, into the concept of "sharing" Mommy. I thought things were going well until the day the baby nurse left. With bags packed, the baby nurse said goodbye and started walking out the door. Suddenly, Sara dashed after her yelling, "You forgot your babies."

HontheP.com

My daughter was watching her dad trying to fix a toy of hers. He couldn't figure it out so she finally said, "I know what's wrong with it." Surprised, he asked, "You do?" In a serious tone she replied, "It's broken." Trying not to laugh, Dad said, "Baby if you're so smart, why aren't you rich?" She replied, "Because the government doesn't know about me yet."

HontheP.com

We were enjoying a family beach day. All six of our kids were swimming and having a blast until lunch when the clouds opened up and it began to pour. Everyone ran for cover except our three-year-old who said, "Hurry everyone, if we get back in the water, we'll stay dry."

HontheP.com

My two sons were outside playing which usually ended with an altercation. This time Matt threw a small rock at Ryan, and Ryan retaliated by squirting super glue at Matt's eye, gluing it shut immediately. The eye doctor said the eye would eventually open. Assuming Ryan had some remorse, I was comforted when he said he'd "take care" of his brother the next day. Little did I know that "care" meant setting his little brother in a chair and charging the neighborhood children admission to see Matt's eye glued shut. I have to say, though, Ryan did split the money with his brother.

Ryan and Matt, 7 & 9
– Georgia

UNCENSORED

We were reading the directions to put a toy car together for Jack, our youngest, and he kept saying "decorations" when he meant to say "directions". Trying to teach him a lesson I said, "No Jack it's di-rec-tions." Five minutes later he was screaming, "Where are the Erections?" I should have stuck with decorations.

Jack, 3 – Florida

I was watching a movie with my two sons one night, when my three year old became agitated. I asked what was wrong and he replied, "Mommy, it won't turn off." "What won't turn off?" I said confused. He stood up in anger and pointed to the "tent" in his underwear. By then my older son was rolling on the floor in fits of laughter, which only enraged my three year old, more.

Trevor, 3 – California

I was playing with my six-year-old son when he started talking about trucks and the trailers they pull behind them. Then out of the blue he asked, "Does Dad have a hooker?"

Ryan, 6 – Michigan

In Vermont every March we have a Town Meeting Day where everyone comes to discuss town issues and elections. My parents were very involved and were always at these usually uneventful meetings. However, one particular meeting my twin sisters had to use the bathroom so my mom, who was busy, let them go alone. They returned very excited and started yelling "Mom look, we got these toys out of the machine in the bathroom and don't know how they work." And there they stood, the center of attention, waving a sanitary pad and tampon in the air for everyone to see.

Anonymous, 8 – Vermont

My two-year-old niece, Tess, had a habit of taking her clothes off. One day, in front of several guests at my nephew's birthday party, Tess removed her new party dress. Half naked she ran in front of her big brother and his friends while they were playing. Frustrated, her brother yelled "Mom, do something...the baby thinks she's a stripper again."

Tess, 2 – Ohio

My daughter is really into Toy Story, so we bought her Toy Story underwear. However, I'm afraid she loved them a little too much. She was so proud of her new panties, she decided to show them off to everyone by shouting, "Who wants to see my Woody?"

Kacie, 3 - Maine

A six-year-old girl I nannied for put on a play for her siblings and me. For some reason, she kept putting the word 'poopy' into the story, which she thought was hilarious. I told her that we wouldn't watch if she continued to use that word. "Fine, fine" she said and began a new story. "Once upon a time...There was a whale with a huge penis..." Suddenly poopy wasn't sounding so bad.

Cosette, 6 – Rhode Island

Stopping to pick my daughter up at Kindergarten, I quickly discovered that the topic of "Show and Tell" that day had been parents' occupations. The teacher pulled me aside and whispered "You might want to explain a little more to your daughter about what you do for a living." I happen to work as a training consultant and often conduct my seminars in motel conference rooms. When I asked the teacher why, she explained, "Well, your daughter told the class she wasn't sure what you did, but you got dressed real pretty and went to work at motels."

Anonymous, 5 – Maryland

I've had a black beard since I was discharged from the Air Force in 1962, so growing up our kids were used to my beard. One day in 1974, when our little girl was about three years old, she walked into the bathroom as my wife was getting out of the shower. Seeing her mother naked for the first time must have surprised our daughter because she commented, "Oh, I never knew you had a beard just like Daddy."

Anonymous, 3 – Utah

My husband and I were giving our son, Gryphon, his first bath, when our two year old, Winnie, wandered in. She watched for a while, and then did a double take, moving in for a closer look. "What's wrong with his bagina?" she demanded in a startled tone.

Winnie, 2 – Maine

One Saturday afternoon we spent the entire day at my parent's house. The weather was warm and the hose was left out because my father had been watering his garden. My daughter, Amy, had fun splashing and playing with the hose all afternoon. The following day we had dinners at my in-laws', who happen to be very conservative and proper people. In the middle of dinner my daughter blurted out "I like to play with Granddad's hose."

Amy, 3 – Delaware

I told my daughter that her aunt was playing hooky from work and was joining us for lunch. When my sister arrived, Shaina ran to her and gave her aunt a big hug exclaiming "Mommy said you were playing hooker today."

Shaina, 5 – Ohio

It was the end of the day when I parked my police van in front of the station. As I gathered my equipment, my K9 partner, Jake, began barking in the back. Nearby a little boy was staring and finally asked, "Is that a dog back there?" I replied, "It sure is." Puzzled, the little boy looked at the back of the van again then asked, "What did he do?"

Anonymous, 4 – New Jersey,

When my son was born, our daughter became very interested in his umbilical cord. I explained that we cleaned it until it eventually fell off which would take about a week. The day it came off she looked puzzled. I couldn't figure out why until she pointed to the baby's penis and asked, "When does that fall off?"

Anonymous, 5 – Kentucky

My son really knows how to embarrass me. He has called random men "Daddy." He pointed to the bottles on the shelves at the local liquor shop and yelled, "Daddy's favorite drink." And when I forgot my PIN number at the ATM, and was frantically trying to remember it, he shouted, "Did you run out of money?"

Anonymous, 4 – Louisiana

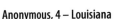

My son has a habit of peeing his pants a little when he gets really scared. One day we were in a restaurant waiting to be seated, and he was holding the beeper device that vibrates when our table was ready in his lap. After about 10 minutes of sitting around, my son suddenly perked up and shouted, "Either my penie is tingling in fear or our table is ready."

Dylan, 9 – Florida

Delaney and Sam were playing together when I overheard Delaney say, "Sam, You can be the castrator." I immediately decided it might be a good time to check and see what game they were playing. Turns out they were playing store, and Sam was the cashier or "castrator".

Delaney & Sam, 3 – Colorado
Peelinganorangewithascrewdriver.blogspot.com

My daughter came up and urgently informed me of the important discovery she had just made. She said "Daddy did you know I have a 'gina, Sissy has a 'gina, Mama has a 'gina and you have peanuts."

Lily, 3 – Massachusetts

Max took off his jammies, removed his diaper, and stood in front of the glass door totally naked as all the neighbors walked their kids to school. And after the morning I had, I don't even care.

Max, 3 – Tennessee

My phone rang, and I heard my wife's hysterical voice on the other end say, "Penis, that's what your daughter called me. Does that Animaniacs cartoon you let her watch call someone a penis?" "No" I replied confidently. "Well, she says that's where she heard it," my wife stated loudly before handing the phone to our daughter. "What did you say to Mommy that got her so upset?" I asked. "I just called her a penis, you know like they do in the cartoon episode about Beethoven." Trying not to laugh, I explained to my daughter, "Until you get older, you should say piano player because when you say it wrong, it's not a nice word."

Cadence, 5 – North Carolina

One night my three kids played a game where they assigned the planets to various family members. I listened as Alyssa claimed Saturn and Phoenix called Venus. They gave their little brother Neptune and so it went. I smiled listening to my children being so cute. That was until Phoenix yelled, "...and Mommy gets Mars and Daddy gets that Anus planet."

Alyssa, 8 – Georgia
www.nixclips.blogspot.com

I was talking to my daughter about buying a new house so we could all have bigger bed-rooms. She seems to have had a few different concerns than me, though because she said "Great now you and Mom will finally have a room big enough so you can both get your own beds, then you won't have to sleep together anymore.

Josie, 5 – Michigan

Out of the blue, my son points to his private area and asked "Mom, what are these balls? Are they full of pee just waiting to get out? Speechless I agreed and hoped I didn't scar him for life.

Bubs, 7 – Ohio

After seeing her dad in his underwear for the first time, my two-year-old daughter drew the most logical conclusion a two year old is capable of...leading her to ask "Did Daddy poop in the front of his pants?"

Zoey, 2 – Kansas

While driving to school one day, my daughter asked, "Mommy, when do you take driving lessons?" I replied, "When you turn sixteen." Frustrated, my daughter responded, "No, I mean when are you going to take driving lessons?"

Izzy, 6 – Tennessee

Maybe I'm just being paranoid, but I swear my son, Max, had a smile on his face when I asked him why he chose "Lake Titicaca" for a social studies paper.

Max, 11 – Michigan

Whenever it was that time of the month, I would say to my daughter, Jenna, "Mommy needs some privacy" as I took a tampon out of the hall closet and went into the bathroom. One particularly was very difficult with the kids, so when my husband returned from work I said "Honey I really need a few minutes of privacy." I was about to head to my bedroom when I noticed Jenna walking towards me with a big smile on her face. She said "Here Mommy, here's your privacy." And she handed me a tampon.

Jenna, 3 – Ohio

It was Regi's first Halloween, and she was excited to yell "Trick or Treat" and receive a very generous treat. As she walked away, my wife interjected, "Now, what do you say?" Regi paused, turned back to the woman in the doorway and said, "More!"

Regi, 3 – South Carolina

school

Sleds

HV2

School bus

I find it amusing that my daughter slept with her toy cell phone next to the bed because she had to "call her boss first thing in the morning." Turns out her "boss" is one of the little girls in her preschool class. When I asked how this selection was made, my daughter reasoned, "Well, it was either Adeline or this boy in my class, and you know...no boy can be the boss of me."

Addison, 5 – North Carolina
Timetomakethebrownies.wordpress.com

My daughter had just finished her first week of school when her grandma asked, "How's school going?" With a dejected look she said "I'm just wasting my time...I can't read, I can't write and they won't let me talk."

Brie, 4 – Massachusetts

I recently asked my students some questions about their parents. Here's my favorite answer. "What did your mom need to know about your dad before she married him?" One first grader replied, "She had to know his background. Like is he a crook? Does he get drunk on beer? She also needed to know whether he makes at least $800 a year and does he say no to drugs and yes to chores?"

1st Grade Teacher – Mississippi

When my son was three years old and starting preschool, we were not rich and had to be careful with every penny. Each day when I packed our son's snack box, I always put in his favorite treat. Since it was expensive, I kept it hidden so he only got the treat in his snack box. He wanted to know how it got there, so his father said that it was by "special magic." Weeks went by, and I began to notice that he had pencils, erasers and things that didn't belong to him in his school bag. When I asked him about it he said, "Oh Mommy, I do the same 'special magic' Daddy does."

Anonymous, 3 – Illinois

My son, Gabe, has a little girl in his class who's infatuated with him. Today she greeted him at the classroom door dressed in full wedding attire and said, "When you get done signing in, then will you marry me?" Like a typical guy he responded, "I am not getting married for a hundred million and two years, and by that time I'll probably be dead."

Gabe, 5 - Michigan

On the first day of Kindergarten, I picked my daughter up and asked how her day went. I was shocked when my daughter summarized her first day saying, "I know I'm going to like Kindergarten, you know why? In class there's no kicking anybody in the front privates because we're all going to be friends." As a Mom, I'm definitely impressed with this school.

Marcie, 5 – Florida

Melinda Roberts

While studying a unit on family trees, one second grader commented, "My grandma is a real-live hillbilly." So I asked the Second Grader what hillbilly meant. Without missing a beat he said, "It means you're from Texas."

2nd Grade Teacher – Indiana

My son, Roger, returned from school one day and asked me if I knew Richard Stands. Uncertain, I asked if that was the name of another student in his school. "No" Roger said, "We are learning the Pledge of Allegiance and at the end it says 'and to the Republic, for Richard Stands.' So who is that guy?"

Roger, 7 Oregon

Ryan was very angry with the rest of his classmates because he didn't get the chair he wanted at lunch. I went over to reason with him and convince him a vacant chair was just as good as the one that had been taken. He was having none of it. Eventually I inquired, "Okay, what's really going on?" He answered, "Well the truth is...I don't like anybody here except for myself"

Ryan, 5 – Arizona

Unpacking school supplies for the first day of school I overheard a student ask, "Why do I need scissors to open a pack of scissors?"

6th Grade Teacher – Oklahoma

My typically sweet baby girl must've been having a rough time at daycare because she suddenly shouted "Shut up and stop crying" to one of her playmates. After being gently corrected by a daycare worker who reminded her "That's not how we talk to our friends, she looked at her playmate and screamed "Shut up please!"

Madelyn, 2 – Pennsylvania

I asked my class "Do you know what a Hobo is?" One little boy immediately responded, "I know I know...it's someone who doesn't have cable TV."

1st Grade Teacher – Michigan

My friend Alice was announcing to her class that she was going to be married. "Do you understand what this means?" she asked her second grade class. One little boy raised his hand and said, "Yes, it means you're getting a roommate."

2nd Grade Teacher – Ohio

As a driver's education teacher at the local high school, I've learned that even the smartest students can get flustered behind the wheel. One day I was giving lessons to three beginners in the car with each scheduled to drive for 30 minutes. The first student completed the time allowed, so I asked him to change places with one of the other students. Gripping the wheel tightly and staring straight ahead as he continued to drive, he asked in a shaky voice, "Should I stop the car first?"

Anonymous, 15 – Pennsylvania

The loud Emergency Broadcast system notification interrupted the TV one morning and Madison asked, "What's that?" I replied, "Oh, that's a test of the emergency broadcast system." Bewildered Madison replied, "Well, how am I supposed to pass that test?"

Madison, 5 – Alabama

Noah is trying to learn French, and he doesn't like it one bit. One day, feeling particularly frustrated, he said, "I just don't see why we can't all speak the same language. It's just not right."

Noah, 5 – South Carolina

On a test I gave to my fourth grade class, I asked "What process is used to make water safe to drink? One Third Grader wrote "Filtration makes water safe because it removes large pollutants like grit, sand, dead sheep and canoeists from the water.

3th Grade Teacher – Mississippi

Many years ago, when I still lived in an apartment, I always talked to the little girl, Tanya, who lived next door. She was wise beyond her years. During election time, eight-year-old Tanya was telling me about a mock election they had at school. I asked Tanya whom she voted for and she replied "Nobody." When I asked why, she explained, "Well, if I voted for one candidate, the other one would be mad at me. And I don't need someone who is going to be president mad at me."

Tanya, 8 – Oregon

I'm the leader of a Girl Scout troop, and one weekend we took a group of fifteen girls to the ballet to see Sleeping Beauty. Two of the girls are cousins who tended to get on each other's nerves, so I sat between them. A few minutes into the ballet, Emmaliegh asked, "When are they going to start talking?" Her cousin Elizabeth replied in an uppity manner "It's ballet...it's a story told by dance." A few minutes later Elizabeth whispered to me so Emmaliegh couldn't hear "So what's happening?"

Emmaliegh and Elizabeth, 9 – Maine

My nephew was having trouble learning the alphabet. Getting frustrated, his mom said, "Ben, do you know why you need to know your ABC's?" "Of course I do" he replied, "So I can learn to text like my sister does."

Ben, 4 – Arizona

"We need money to give to the school for the salami," my twins said. Confused, I asked, "Why does your class need salami?" They looked at me like I was stupid and explained, "No, we need to give money to the school so they can give it to the people hurt in the salami." Finally, I got it, they were talking about the tsunami.

HontheP.com

My daughter's 5th grade class was discussing the qualifications needed to be a U.S. President – 35 years or older and a natural born citizen. A girl in class complained that the "natural born" requirement prevented many capable people from being President. Upon further questioning, the girl explained that "it was unfair because a natural born citizen is in no way more qualified to lead the country than one born by c-section."

HontheP.com

AGE

My niece, Shyann, was having a princess birthday party – no boys allowed. Her younger brother, Chandlor, became upset hearing non-stop about the party he wasn't invited to. The day of the party he couldn't bear watching all of the giggly girls having fun. So he marched into the party announcing to his mom "When it's my birthday I want a Nerf gun party, and I want the girls to be the targets."

Chandlor, 5 – Indiana

When Patrick and I were walking, we passed a very old man walking slowly in the opposite direction. After we went by him Patrick asked innocently "Mom, why is his skin too big for his body?"

Patrick, 5 – Michigan

I was driving in my car with my son listening to oldies on the radio. My son asked me why I listened to old music, and I told him because I was old. He thought about this for a moment then he asked, "Did you know Christopher Columbus because it could really help me out on my social studies report."

Kenny, 8 – Florida

After watching an old movie, my son turned me and asked inquisitively, "Were you alive when everything was black and white outside?"

Cory, 7 – Nebraska

It was my older daughter's birthday, so my three year old wanted to know when it would be her turn to have a birthday. I patiently explained that first it was big sister's birthday, then Daddy's birthday later in the month, Mommy's birthday in two months, her little sister's birthday after that, and finally her birthday four months later. Clearly upset she cried, "I'll be too old to have a birthday by then."

Anonymous, 3 Maryland

On my 40th birthday I overheard my daughter say to her little brother, "Buddy, it's not that Albertson's doesn't have that many candles. It's just that if we light them all at once, we'll burn the house down. That's why we're making Mommy cupcakes.

Mackenzie, 7 – Utah

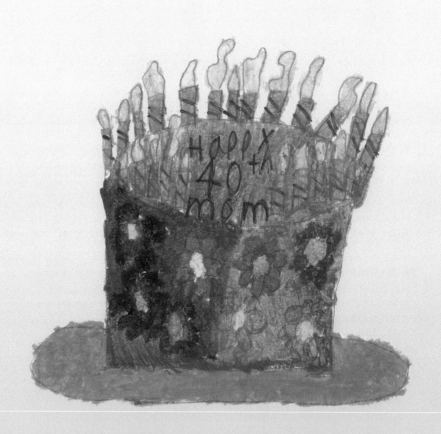

My neighbor was throwing a sweet sixteen party for her daughter, Stacy. After fighting with her little brother, Andy, all morning Andy told his mom the party should be renamed sour sixteen because Stacy had been a sour puss all day.

Andy, 10 – Ohio

I recently quizzed my eight year old, "What does benign mean?" He confidently told me, "Benign is what you will be after you be eight."

Anonymous, 8 – Maine

A friend asked my daughter, "How old are you?" She responded with pride, "I'm three pounds."

Anonymous, 3 – Iowa

I was driving down the street one Sunday afternoon with my four-year-old son Jonathon when he asked, "Do you remember when I was a baby?" "Yes, of course" I answered. He then asked, "Daddy, what was my name when I was a baby?"

Jonathon, 4 – Illinois

During my husband's birthday, my three year old asked how old everyone was. I told her that her older sister is twelve, Daddy just turned thirty five, and her younger sister is almost one. She then asked how old I was. I hesitated and then replied, twenty seven. She looked at me very seriously and exclaimed, "Again?"

Anonymous, 3 – Maryland

Out of the blue my daughter asked, "Momma, can you blow a bubblegum bubble?" I replied, "Of course." My daughter continued, "Can you teach me?" "Sure." I said. In a concerned voice my daughter added, "But not until I'm seven okay? It's just too much pressure for a six-year-old."

Madison, 6 – Alaska
Justliketheanimal.blogspot.com

JANUARY 2012

SUNDAY	MONDAY	TUESDAY	WEDNESDAY	THURSDAY	FRIDAY	SATURDAY
1 NEW YEAR		3	4	5	6	7
8		10	11	12	13	14
15		18	19	20	21	
22	23	24	25	26	27	28
29	30	31				

STAR

My son Eythen says "Mom, I know what I wanna' be when I grow up. On Fridays, I will drive a train. And on Mondays, I'm gonna' be famous like Justin Bieber."

HontheP.com

I took our kids to a small festival at Old Fort Bliss over the weekend. The museum had exhibits that showed what it was like in 1857 without things like indoor bathrooms and electricity. I explained to my kids that this is how people lived long, long ago. Apparently, they didn't quite catch the long ago part because my eight year old said in amazement "So this is what it was like when you were a kid Mom? You had it rough."

Caitlin, 8 – Texas

I was looking at my three-year-old daughter and wondered what her future would be like. I said out loud to her "I wonder what you'll be when you're older." Without hesitation she replied "Four."

Lani, 4 – Michigan

GRANDPARENTS

Grandma was having an overnight with her Granddaughter, Emily. Before bed, Emily saw a mud pack on her grandma's face and asked what it was. Grandma explained that it was a treatment for her face and would keep her skin young and soft. After touching her grandma's face Emily asked innocently, "Is it working?"

Emily, 3 – Georgia

As I frantically waved away a pesky fly with a white dishtowel to no avail, my granddaughter observed, "Maybe he thinks you're surrendering."

Olive, 6 – South Carolina

My daughter was sitting on her grandpa's lap staring at his wrinkled face. "How did you get all of those lines on your face, Papa?" she asked. Joking he said "I drew them on myself." Carefully examining his face turning it from side to side, Shaina declared, "You did a good job. I don't see any pen marks."

Shaina, 6 – Ohio

Shortly after my second child was born, I explained to my son that he needed to put his toys in a different place so his baby sister wouldn't choke on them. One afternoon after leaving him at the house with his grandmother for several hours, I returned from shopping to find a small, red Power Ranger in the baby's toy basket. Initially, he tried in earnest to pin the infraction on his grandmother. When that didn't work, he stormed out of the room shouting, "I don't need people here babysitting me if they're just going to get me in trouble."

Griffin, 6 – North Carolina
Timetomaketthebrownies.wordpress.com

My granddaughter, Hannah, asked me what my childhood was like, so I told her, "We used to skate outside on a pond; I often played on a swing made from a tire that hung from our front yard tree; I rode my pony; and I picked raspberries in the woods." Hannah was wide-eyed, taking it all in. At last Hannah said, "I sure wish I'd gotten to know you sooner."

Hannah, 6 – North Carolina

I volunteered for an organization that delivers lunches to elderly shut-ins, and I used to take my four-year-old daughter with me on my afternoon rounds. She was always intrigued by the various "appliances" of old age especially the canes, walkers and wheelchairs. One day I found her staring at a pair of false teeth soaking in a glass. As I braced myself for the inevitable barrage of questions, I was surprised when she whispered excitedly, "The Tooth Fairy will never believe this."

Anonymous, 4 – New Jersey

A friend of mine was always scolding her little girl, Jodi, for not listening to her, explaining how she must always do what her mommy says. So one day, Jodi heard her mom and grandma having a disagreement. Deciding to settle the matter herself, she told her mom, "Remember you have to do what your mommy says."

Jodi, 5 – Iowa

My granddaughter asked me, "Granny, how old are you?" I said to her, "I'm too old to remember." With a look of satisfaction she said, "Do what I do and look in the back of your underpants. Mine say 5 to 6."

HontheP.com

We were having a welcome home party for my dad who had surgery on his eye. Noticing the bandage, my niece looked concerned and asked, "What happened to your eye Papa?" Teasing, he said, "Grandma hit me." Looking straight at her grandma, Chelsie scolded, "I hope you got a time out."

Chelsie, 7 – Wisconsin

After looking closely at his grandma's face one day, my son commented, "Granny, you know Mom has an iron that takes the wrinkles out of everything."

Jessica, 9 – Nevada

My mom, my daughter and I were having dinner at Applebee's when my mom announced that "Mother Nature" was calling. Getting up from her chair to visit the bathroom, Jodi whispered "But I didn't hear Grandma's cell phone ring."

Jodi, 6 – Ohio

I had to listen to my two-year-old son scream hysterically for an hour in the car because my iPod would not "call Grammy."

Max, 2 – Minnesota

One weekend I took my grandson to our cabin in the woods. In the evening, he became upset because he began noticing lots of mosquitoes. Trying to make him feel better I said, "If we turn the lights off, and stay in the cabin we won't attract them." It seemed to work for a few minutes until my grandson screamed, "It's no use...now they're coming after us with flashlights."

Anonymous, 8 – Massachusetts

When my daughter was two years old she would place her hand on top of her head every time we went outside. As she was playing in the sandbox one day with one hand securely on top of her head, I asked her why she did that. She replied, "I don't want my hair to blow away like Grampy's did."

Anonymous, 2 – South Carolina

My neighbor had not seen her grandson in a while. When he came to visit, she said, "My goodness. You're growing like a weed. What is your mom feeding you?" Without hesitating, Chris replied "Cupcakes."

Chris, 6 – Ohio

My mother toured the Louvre in 1987 with her seven-year-old granddaughter. When they went in search of a restroom, she found the line to the ladies room very long. Rather than wait patiently, she opted to use the men's room where there was no line, telling her granddaughter to guard the door and not allow anyone in. When Grandma stepped out of the men's room, there was a gentleman standing next to her granddaughter who said "Your granddaughter wouldn't let me in the men's room, and when I asked why, she explained, 'You see my grandmother has five sons, and she knows how to go standing up.'"

Josie, 6 – Maine

My daughters were sitting across from my mother and me in a diner when I noticed my eldest daughter staring at us. She pointed at my mom and then me and simply said, "Before and After."

Anonymous, 13 – Oregon

My son, Cullen, recently said, "Grandpa is the smartest man on earth. He teaches me good things, but I don't see him enough to get as smart as him."

Cullen, 5 – New Hampshire

When my daughter was five, I started tracing my family heritage, and explained to her that our family was half Irish, part Dutch, and a tiny bit German. My daughter shot back, "No, I'm not. Grandma says I am half Angel and a lot Princess."

Shaina, 5 – Ohio

My grandma used to call grandpa, "The Bull" because he was stubborn. One day while talking on the phone Grandma told her friend to come over to "shoot the bull." After she hung up I pleaded, "Please don't shoot Grandpa."

Anonymous, 6 – Nevada

My daughter was a chocoholic and would eat sweets instead of meals. After her fourth mini candy bar, I told her that she had plenty and should put the bag away. Pouting as she stomped away, she grabbed the telephone and said, "I am going to tell Grandma you made me cry."

Shaina, 6 – Ohio

My grandson sleeps over from time to time. This particular morning I was distracted as I busily made him pancakes and sausages for breakfast and drank my coffee. I thought the coffee tasted odd, and when I got towards the bottom of the mug, I noticed three of those tiny green army men. I said to my Grandson, "Honey, what are the army men doing in my coffee?" He replied, "Grandma, it says on TV that the best part of waking up is soldiers in your cup."

Anonymous – Oregon

I was reading my granddaughter a bedtime story. As I read, she reached up to touch the wrinkles on my face (I have a few), and then she touched her cheeks. She then asked, "Grandpa, did God make you?" I replied, "Yes sweetheart, God made me a long, long time ago." She then asked, "Did God make me too?" I answered, "Yes God made you just a little while ago." Feeling the wrinkles on my face again she observed, "God's getting much better at it isn't he?"

Anonymous, 4 – New Jersey

I didn't know if my granddaughter had learned her colors yet, so I decided to test her. I would point out something and ask what color it was. Her answers were always correct. It was fun for me, so I kept doing it. Finally, she headed to the door exhausted saying, "Grandma, I think you should try to figure some of these out yourself."

Anonymous, 5 – New York

My granddaughter was diligently pounding away on my computer. When I asked what she was doing, she replied, "I'm writing a story. Amused I continued, "What's the story about?" She replied in a huff, "I don't know, I can't read."

Cadence, 3 – North Carolina

While eating at a family restaurant, my nephew grew restless and started running around. Grandma, who is very proper, had enough of her grandson's bad behavior and said to him, "You are driving me up a wall." To which he replied nonchalantly "Well Grandma, what goes up must come down."

Jay, 6 – Iowa

I saw my granddaughter trying to open a medicine bottle and informed her that it was "child proof." With an astounded look on her face she asked, "How does the bottle know it's me?"

Brittany, 4 – South Carolina

While coloring with my granddaughter, she looked at me sweetly and said "Nana, that's my favorite color yellow." Confused I said, what color yellow is that?" expecting her to point at a crayon. Instead she pointed at my teeth.

Blair, 5 – New York

My daughter Shaina recently asked, "Grandpa, why don't you have a job like my Daddy does?" "I used to go to work, but now I'm retired" said Grandpa. "Do you know what retired means?" he asked her. "Yes, it means you're too tired to work anymore."

Shaina, 5 – Ohio

fries

GROSS

My one-year-old son woke up from his nap, soaking wet so I decided to strip him down right there in his crib. I turned my back for a second and walked over to get clean clothing and diapers thinking what could go wrong. Suddenly I heard loud laughter and turned the corner to find my adorable son peeing through the bars between his crib while my dog caught it mid-stream.

Anonymous, 1 – New Hampshire

As I sit in the living room listening, I can hear my husband talking to our son. My husband says, "Quiet I think I hear ducks." To which our son responds, "Dad you're suppose to tell me to pull your finger first."

Jerry, 5 – Illinois
Thenightowlmama.com

My son, Silas, decided his "stink" had come to a point where even he had to admit deodorant was necessary. Unfortunately, his deodorant using phase was short lived. I recently learned the reason when he told his brother and sister "I can't do honking noises with my armpit when I put deodorant on. So I stopped using it." At least he has his priorities straight.

Silas, 10 – South Carolina

My nephew, who lives in Los Angeles and is unfamiliar with the sights and smells of our lovely rural valley, came to visit with his parents. Driving by a large cattle ranch, my nephew began to cry in pain. Alarmed by the unusual outburst his mother asked what was wrong. My nephew replied, "Mommy I've got poop in my nose. Can you get it out?"

Anonymous, 3 – California

After a great day with my son, I took him to Walmart to pick out a toy. While in aisle 5, which happened to be filled with people, my son lets out the grossest and loudest toot I've ever smelled or heard. "Mommy, I can't believe you just did that," he screamed loudly. I was so embarrassed that I scolded him abruptly. An older man who was standing nearby laughed and said, "It's okay it happens. There's no need to blame the little guy."

Jacob, 7 – Virginia

My daughter was just finishing up toilet training when one day I noticed the roll of toilet paper was empty after she left the bathroom. I told her next time to let me know when that happened because "Mommy didn't always notice right away when there was no toilet paper." "Don't worry about it," she replied, "I can always use my hands."

Ellie, 2 – California

After a large Thanksgiving dinner at a friend's house, my husband excused himself to use the bathroom. When he was done, he sprayed the room with lemon air freshener that was on the counter. Our son, Elias, ran upstairs to check on his dad who was walking out of the bathroom. Elias sniffed the air and then asked, "What's that smell?" Dad replied "its lemon." Confused Elias said, "You pooped a lemon?"

Elias, 3 – Pennsylvania

At a family gathering James was busy playing with his cousins when he passed gas in front of everyone. Surprised, his mom asked him what he should say. James smiled, grabbed his behind, and said, "Excuse my butt, please."

James, 3 – Ohio

I hate it when my kids are sick. However, it's fairly hard not to laugh when your nine year old gets the flu and pleads between dry heaves, "I can't take this anymore. We have to find a cure...and we have to do it now."

Griffin, 9 – North Carolina
Timetomakethebrownies.wordpress.com

My daughter stayed home sick from school, so I suggested we color to give her something to do. Morgan was busy drawing a flower when I said, "Do you want me to draw a picture of you?" Excitedly she replied, "Yes, draw me throwing up. And don't forget to draw my puke bucket."

Morgan, 3 – New Jersey

Years ago, I was teaching first grade. As a special treat, we ordered pizza for the kids at lunch. After lunch, we had circle time and one of the little guys in the front passed gas. I usually ignore such events so as not to draw attention to the student. But, this time, the scent was nauseatingly thick, and I couldn't help but comment. I looked at the little boy who committed the offense and said, "No more pizza for you." He looked at me and responded, "But it's not the pizza that stinks. It's the fart."

1st Grade Teacher – Florida

My nephew is a huge Ghandolf the Wizard fan, so of course he wanted a cloak just like the wizard. Since money was tight, we gave him Grandpa's old, grey t-shirt telling him it was a magical Ghandolf cloak. He was so excited he ran around the house in circles jumping and giggling. Suddenly we heard a loud noise, then my nephew grabbed his butt and cried, "Oh no...I just pooped my magic cloak."

Anonymous, 3 – Pennsylvania

My son came to me very upset on day saying, "Daddy, when you cut my fingernails too short, it's harder to pick my boogers."

Anonymous, 3 – Connecticut

Like all Moms I try to instill in my kids the importance of sharing...only my oldest son has figured out a sure-fire way to avoid this sibling duty. One day while in the kitchen my daughter came to me in tears yelling, "Mitchel took my squirt gun." From the other room, I heard Mitchel defending himself, "I offered to give it back." When I asked my daughter if this was true, she cried, "Yes, but he put it down his pants." Turns out once an item goes down Mitchel's pants it loses its desirability.

Michael 10 – Michigan

My son told me, "Dad I'm playing with my walker outside." Confused, I asked him "What's a walker?" He replied, "I created it. It's a fly whose wings are torn off so it has to walk."

Anonymous, 5 – Montana

My son fell off the bed after pretending to be Superman and got a small gash on his eyebrow. As blood streamed down his face, I tried to stay calm and stop the bleeding. My son brushed the blood from his face and looked at his hand in amazement. Bracing myself for the inevitable cries of agony, I was dumbfounded when he held up his blood stained hand and said excitedly, "Look Mom...red it's my favorite color."

Trevor, 3 – New York

My dad told my daughter, "I have a frog in my throat." Concerned, my daughter said "Grandpa, I think you better go to the bathroom and poop that frog out."

Rachel, 6 – South Carolina

"Mommy I'm bored" my daughter whined one day. "Why don't you write or draw in your diary?" I suggested. "Yeah, great idea Mom, I love my diarrhea."

Maddie, 7 – Utah
Obviouslymarvelous.blogspot.com

While riding in the car with my oldest son who was seven, we entered into a deep discussion about how the earth rotates creating day and night. Afterward, my son grew quiet. Thinking he was pondering the heavy concepts we just discussed, I asked him what he was thinking about. He replied, "Mom, you know what? I just figured out that if you scratch your butt through your underwear your finger won't stink."

Anonymous, 7 – Mississippi

I looked over at my three-year-old and asked, "What are you doing?" She replied casually, "Picking my nose." I thought she would take the hint when I said, "Are you supposed to be doing that?" Instead, she replied defiantly, "Are you supposed to be watching?"

www.HontheP.com

My granddaughter was visiting when I said to her, "I think the dog has a peppermint candy cane stuck to her rear." I thought she would help me get it off. Instead, she took one look and said, "At least it will taste good when she licks her butt now."

www.HontheP.com

My son came screaming out of the bathroom to tell me he'd dropped his toothbrush in the toilet. My son watched as I fished out the toothbrush and threw it in the garbage. He stood there thinking for a moment, then ran to my bathroom and came out with my toothbrush. He gave it to me and said with a charming smile, "We better throw this one out too 'cause it fell in the toilet a few days ago."

Anonymous, 5 – Wisconsin

My friends were having a baby and didn't know the sex of the child. They asked their three-year-old daughter if she wanted a little brother or sister. She thought for a second and said with a smile, "I want french fries."

Anonymous, 3 – Louisiana

When I was pregnant, my daughter, Audrey, pointed to my chest and said "boobies." So I asked "And what is going to come from them?" "Milk" she replied. "That's right, sweetie and who is the milk for?" I asked. Audrey answered, "Baby Jamie's going to drink the milk, and I'm going to put it on my cereal."

Audrey, 3 – Maryland
www.binkertation.com

I was eight and a half months pregnant and swimming with my daughter. She pointed at my stomach and asked, "Aren't you going to drown him?"

Anonymous, 6 – Kansas

Curious my son asked, "Can boys have babies?" I told him "No only girls." "Girls get fat when they're going to have a baby right?" he asked. "Yes they get a lot bigger" I responded. "So when are you going to have your baby?"

Hunter, 6 – Kentucky

I was pregnant with my second child. I was midway through the pregnancy when I let my six-year-old, Tommy, feel the baby moving in my tummy. He acted unimpressed and didn't say much. A few days later, Tommy's teacher took me aside and said she had asked Tommy, "Whatever has become of that baby brother or sister you're expecting." Bursting into tears he replied, "I think Mommy ate him."

Tommy, 6 – Virginia

Our new baby was about to arrive and would be taking over our older daughter's, crib. We bought Gretchen a big girl bed, but she had difficulty adjusting to the new set-up. During nap time, I noticed Gretchen was missing from her new big girl bed. After a few minutes of searching, I found her lying in her old, baby crib fast asleep. When she awoke from her nap, I asked her why she was in the baby's crib and not her big girl bed. Without hesitation she replied, "I was just visiting."

Gretchen, 2 – Wisconsin

My niece, Jessica, was so excited about her new baby brother. She called her grandma (who had not yet seen the baby) to tell her all about him. Her grandma asked what the new baby looked like. She replied, "Oh Grandma, he's wrinkled and bald just like Grandpa."

Jessica, 8 – California

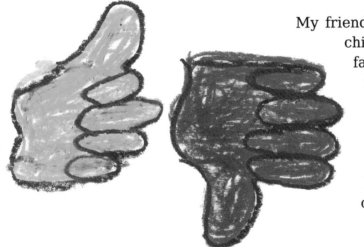

My friend found out she was having her sixth child, so she and her husband called a family meeting to announce the blessing. "Kids, we're going to have a new baby," Dad said. Everyone was quiet after receiving the unexpected news. So Mom added, "Do you have any questions?" Jillian, the second child, blurted out "Do we get to vote on this one?"

Jillian, 13 – Ohio

I announced to my first grade class "I just want the class to know that I'm going to have a baby." One little girl whose own mother was already well along in her pregnancy raised her hand and asked, "My daddy put a baby inside my mommy...did he put one in you too?"

Kelly, 7 – Missouri

My younger daughter was expecting her first child and began asking about child birth and delivery. My grandson listened intently and finally said, "Auntie, why don't you just spit the baby out...that way it won't hurt."

Anonymous, 7 – Maryland

I announced to my daughter, Lori, that her aunt just had a baby and that it looked just like her uncle. She replied, "You mean he has a mustache?"

Lori, 5 – South Carolina

After the birth of our second baby, my husband brought our older daughter, Gretchen, to the hospital to visit the baby and me. My roommate had delivered a baby girl too, and both babies were in the room. Thinking she had a choice, Gretchen took a good look at both infants in their bassinets and pointed to my roommate's baby saying, "Mommy, let's take this one."

Gretchen, 3 – Ohio

My two children, Jack and Isla, know the broad strokes about reproduction, mostly just who can have babies (girls) and who cannot (boys). Jack may have gotten the wrong message, however, because one day he says "Isla, can you push out some babies so there are some more people to play with around here?"

Jack, 4 – Washington
Aggraygate.blogspot.com

The only experience my older son had with pregnancy was what he learned from his Grandpa the vet who often delivered litters of animals. After delivering my second child, I took my eldest son to see his new baby brother in the hospital nursery with all the other newborns. I was a bit surprised, however, when his only question was, "Mom, are all these ours?"

Luke, 3 – Virginia

My cousin recently had a baby. Upon arriving home, she explained to new big sister, Emily, how she had to be careful with her tiny sister because the baby could not hold her head up and her neck could bend backwards. When a friend came to visit, Emily immediately told her, "You have to be careful...the baby breaks."

Emily, 3 – California

We were Christmas shopping with my daughter who became tired and fussy after a while. She begged me to pick her up. Tired myself because I was 7 months pregnant with a big belly, I tried to explain "I'm already holding your baby sister or baby brother in my tummy so it's too hard for me to pick you up." Crying she demanded, "Then put them down."

Gretchen, 2 – Ohio

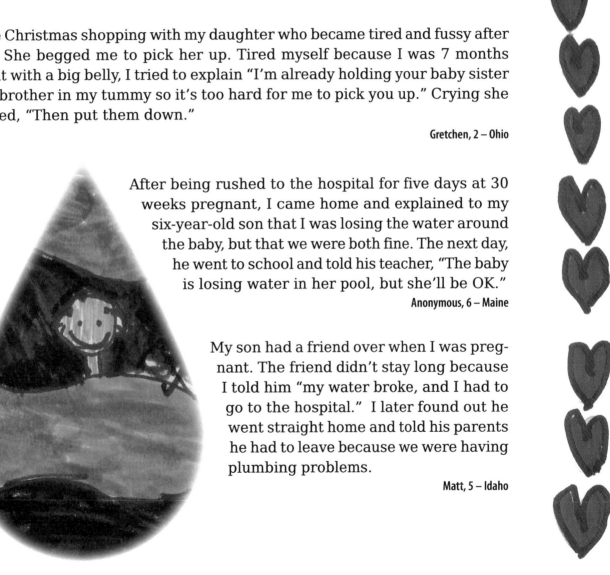

After being rushed to the hospital for five days at 30 weeks pregnant, I came home and explained to my six-year-old son that I was losing the water around the baby, but that we were both fine. The next day, he went to school and told his teacher, "The baby is losing water in her pool, but she'll be OK."

Anonymous, 6 – Maine

My son had a friend over when I was pregnant. The friend didn't stay long because I told him "my water broke, and I had to go to the hospital." I later found out he went straight home and told his parents he had to leave because we were having plumbing problems.

Matt, 5 – Idaho

SHOCKING

I apologize to my daughter's fifth grade teacher who asked the class during geography, if anyone knew where "the poles" were located, and got the following answer from my daughter, "Vegas."

Molly, 9 – Michigan

A friend of mine has a daughter with stunning red hair. There's nothing subtle about it. When she was little, people would constantly stop and ask, "Where did you get that red hair?" Her mom, who's a brunette, decided to coach her to answer, "It runs in the family." The next time a stranger came up to her and asked the question, Mom stood back and quietly told her daughter, "Go ahead, remember what we practiced saying?" So her daughter replied, "I got it from a friend of the family."

Aimee, 6 – Kansas

I was at the Costco checkout line with my three-year-old, Hunter, who was just learning to be potty trained. There were two "manly" men behind us buying Super Bowl provisions. They engaged in a conversation with Hunter as I unloaded the cart. Suddenly I noticed the two men awkwardly looking in every direction but at my son trying in vain to ignore him as he pointed at them. Immediately I called Hunter closer and asked him what he said. Hunter replied "I only said you have a penie and you have a penie."

Hunter, 3 – Pennsylvania

While visiting a relative in the hospital, my son noticed an elderly man in the hallway. "Mom, doesn't the doctor think that man is too old to have a wheelchair with a jetpack on it?" my son said as he pointed to the old man in a wheelchair connected to oxygen tanks.

Anonymous, 7 – Virginia

Like all parents, we taught our kids about "stranger danger" though I think my oldest daughter learned the lesson all too well. One cold winter day while at the mall, my daughter wouldn't put her coat on, wouldn't leave, and threw a tantrum. My husband finally carried her off to the car over his shoulder while she kicked and screamed the whole way. Outside by the car she began yelling "I don't want to go...this isn't my dad...don't take me." About an hour after we got home we received a knock at the door. It was two policemen asking if they could speak to us about a kidnapping.

Emma, 8 – Michigan

When my daughter wouldn't stop bothering my son, I overheard him shout at her "Leave me alone...I'm constipating." (Concentrating)

Janelle & Mike, 9 and 6 – Ohio

I recently asked my third grade students, "What happens when a boy reaches puberty?" One of my students confidently responded, "He says goodbye to boyhood and looks forward to adultery."

2nd Grade Teacher – California

My oldest son was on the couch with our crying baby who was hungry. I was busy for the moment with our middle son when I heard the oldest yell "I did it." I looked over in shock as I saw the baby's face smashed against my son's chest. He proudly informed me "I'm feeding the baby." After rescuing the poor infant from any further trauma, I had a little talk with my son about who could and who couldn't breast feed a baby.

Jack, 5 – Massachusetts

After coming home from a birthday party, my niece looked into her goody bag and asked, "Mom, can I have a bite of my Sweet-Ass Fish?" (Swedish Fish)

Gracie, 6 – Pennsylvania

We were reading about sea creatures, so at the end of the book I pretended to be an octopus. I told my preschool class, "I'm an Octopus and I'm going to wrap you in my tentacles." One boy in my class became a little defensive and replied, "Hey you better watch out, or I am going to wrap my testicles around you."

PreK Teacher – New York

We were waiting for my husband at his office. To occupy the kids, I took them to the conference room with the dry-erase board. The kids began drawing on the board, and I was touched when my five-year-old son said "Mom I'm drawing a picture of you." After looking at the circle with one dot in the middle that looked suspiciously like a boob, I said to my son "But honey I have two eyes not one…and you forgot my nose and mouth." He smiled sweetly and said "But Mom I wasn't drawing your face."

Tyler, 5 – Nevada

I asked my fourth grade class "What does a bank need to get a mortgage for a home loan?" One of my students raised his hand and answered, "They insist you're well endowed."

4th Grade Teacher – New York

I was saying goodnight to my son and noticed he had his hand in his pants. When I asked him what he was doing he replied nonchalantly "Checking." Confused I asked, "What are you checking for?" My son replied, "I'm checking to make sure both my balls are there." I assured him that he didn't need to worry about such a thing. Still concerned he replied "But every time I go for a physical, the doctor always checks to make sure they're there, so I figured if he thinks they can get lost, I better keep checking on them." I was speechless.

Drew, 8 – Oregon

My co-worker, Kathy, underwent emergency surgery and missed her seven-year-old daughter's parent-teacher conference. When she finally went, Kathy sensed that the teacher was uncomfortable. Kathy told the teacher she missed the conference due to her surgery for gall stones. With a sign of relief, the teacher said, "Oh that makes more sense. Jessica said you couldn't come because you were stoned and had to go to the hospital."

Jessica, 7 - Colorado

At the supermarket, we saw an extremely large body builder type of guy. Since my son was being potty trained, he was into body parts and how they functioned, especially the private ones. So he took one look at this huge, muscular guy and shouted "Look at that big guy, his penis must be huge."

Patrick, 3 – Minnesota

My son Aaron was two and a half. He said, "Dad, you wanna play with my cars?" I said, "Sure." He said, "O.K., I'll be the 'Cordavette' and you be the idiot who is driving too slow."

Aaron, 2 – CO

My daughter was telling me a long, drawn out story about something I already had heard about from her teacher. Toward the end she said "And do you know what happened next?" In the mood to tease her, I said "I know exactly what happened next" and I went on to complete the story. My daughter just stared in wonderment at me and gasped, "Mommy, you must be psycho or something." (Psychic)

Anonymous, 8 – California

My son broke his arm, and after his cast was taken off, we had to visit the orthopedist a few times to make sure it was healing properly. When I picked up my son from school, the teacher pulled me aside to let me know he told the entire class at show and tell all about his visit to the "ortho-penis."

Luke, 6 – Colorado

My five-year-old child was riding in the car when he became frustrated trying to make his toy work. "Oh drats," he yelled. Hearing such a funny expression, I commented, "That's what Charlie Brown says." "Who's Charlie Brown?" my son asked. "He's a little boy who's in a cartoon," I replied. "Well the only Charlie I know is Charlie Sheen" my son concluded.

Anonymous, 5 – Colorado
Betsybrownbraun

My husband is a Republican and I'm a Democrat which explains why our daughter recently said, "Mom, I can't remember the name of those people who steal money." I replied, "Do you mean robbers?" "No, you know...the really bad people who are taking our money. It starts with a D, I think." Unsure I answered, "Democrats?" My daughter replied, "Yeah, that's it!"

Blair, 6 – Michigan

 "Who drew a colorful face on the closet wall?" I asked my daughter accusingly. She cautiously replied, "What will happen to the person who confesses?"

Anonymous, 6 – Kansas

When my son was three, we were at the grocery store, and there was a lady in her military uniform shopping beside us with her child. My son was looking intently at her with the most disturbed look on his face. Finally, he blurted out "Mommy, GI Joe is a girl, and she has a baby." I thought I was going to die until the military lady replied, "No, I'm better than GI Joe."

Samuel, 3 – New Jersey

DEATH

I went to visit my nephew. The minute I stepped out of the car, he came running over to me and took my hand saying excitedly "Come on...I have to show you the turtle Grandma ran over." So he brings me to a bucket with a dead, totally crushed baby turtle and explains, "Part of it went to Heaven, part of it didn't."

Joshua, 5 – Maine

I took my daughters to Pet Smart to just look at the fish. A sales lady walked up and asked if she could get a fish for us. My daughter replied, "Do you have any dead ones? We kill them anyway."

Briana, 6 – North Carolina

My husband was walking with our five-year-old daughter when our elderly neighbor told him her husband, Jim, passed away. My husband gave his condolences saying he was "Sorry." Months later, we saw Mrs. L planting flowers and my daughter said "Awww poor Mrs. L. Why did Dad kill her husband?" Shocked I asked, "Why would you think that?" My daughter replied, "Because Daddy said he was sorry."

Anonymous, 5 – New Jersey

"That's the place they put people that the doctors can't fix anymore," my son said pointing to the cemetery.

Jason, 3 – Massachusetts

Grandpa, who stayed in touch with his grandson by texting, died suddenly when our son was five. Trying to approach the matter delicately, we explained that "Grandpa was picking up Grandma, and they were going to Heaven." Our son thought for a moment, then he replied, "Well when he gets there, can he text me?"

Kyle, 5 – New Hampshire

After what felt like a week of thunder storms, my son came to me very concerned saying "I need to get new holy water for Grandpa's grave. It rained and the holiness is all thinned out."

Eliot, 5 – Ohio

Lani had become increasing interested in death and how to get to Heaven. One day she asked me, "When your Dada died, did he drive to Heaven?" I replied, "No." To which she responded excitedly, "I know, he flew on a kite to get there."

Lani, 4 – Michigan

We drove from Florida to Utah, which was a very long trip. We finally made it to Dinosaur National Monument which my son had been waiting to see. A few minutes into the tour, my son put his hands on his hips and scolded me, "It took you so long to get here that now all the dinosaurs are dead."

Jake, 4 – Utah
Jonbonjovious.blogspot.com

I took my daughters to the pet store to see the fish. A sales lady walked up and asked if she could get a fish for us. My older daughter replied, "Do you have any dead ones? We kill them anyway."

Brianna, North Carolina – 6

Sitting around the dinner table one evening, my six-year-old daughter looked at me and stated, "I know what a cemetery is Mommy." Surprised, I said, "You do?" She then replied, "Yes, it is where you take dead people and plant them."

Naomi, 6 – Tennessee

On the news they were talking about a hurricane passing through Florida. My son gasped, "I sure hope God is OK." Shocked I asked "What does God have to do with this?" He responded, "Well God lives in Florida." So I asked "What makes you think that?" My son smile and replied "Don't you know Mommy that all old people live in Florida? They expire there." (Retire)

Anonymous – 5
www.livinglifewithraandfms.wordpress.com

When my youngest son was five, he helped me install a new floor in our kitchen. He worked hard nailing the plywood, putting down the glue, and installing the new linoleum. He did a great job and was such a good helper, but I could tell something was bothering him. Finally, he asked "Dad is this gonna' be in for a long, long, time?" I told him "Well, I certainly hope so. Why?" With an obvious look of disapproval, he said, "'Cause when you die, I might wanna' change it."

Billy, 5 – Minnesota

I had a conversation with my son, Chandlar, recently about death. Chandlar said, "I don't want to be cremated when I die." Not sure where this was going I replied "Okay." He continued "What about you?" Thinking...Wow am I actually having this conversation now, I decided to be practical and responded, "I want to be cremated so you won't have to spend as much money on me." My son replied reassuringly "Don't worry about it. I'll be a millionaire from my job chasing tornadoes by then. I'll be a hot shot meteorologist, so I'll be able to afford not to cremate you."

Chandlar, 8 – Wyoming

I was driving with my daughter, Addison, when she asked, "Mommy, is Cooper playing with Shadow in heaven?" They were my neighbor's puppy and our eight-month-old lab that met their heartbreaking demise via vehicular dogicide this past spring. Trying to sound comforting I replied, "Yes, baby." Addison continued "And when we move to the new house, we can get a new puppy and put up a gate right?" I replied "Sure why not." So Addison said "Well, that's good because I'd like this puppy to live to get a little older. Then we can take it out and let it get hit by a car." Is this the lesson she learned about getting older? Now I'm scared that at a certain point, she'll decide I'm old and say "Let's wheel her out to the middle of I-95. If Mom makes it, she makes it. If not, it's her time to go."

Addison, 5 – North Carolina

"Mom, I love you so much...when you die I'm going to bury you outside my window."

Stephen, 3 – North Carolina

Emily was playing in her room when suddenly I heard sirens. An ambulance stopped in front of my house and the paramedic said "We have a report of a dead baby at this location." I raced upstairs with the paramedics right behind me...and there we found Emily in my bed on the phone with the 911 operator while she held her "dead" cabbage patch doll in her arms.

Emily, 5 – Georgia
Grammyslists.com

My sister-in-law was babysitting my son. She was having trouble getting him to eat something healthy. Never having any kids of her own, Dawn assumed she could use reason and explained how junk food was unhealthy and that she was a vegetarian. "What's a vegetarian?" asked Jake. "It means I only eat vegetables" my sister-in-law replied. Jake thought for a minute and then said, "Well, that explains it, I'm a junk food-etarian, I only eat junk food."

Jake, 7 – Ohio

My son asked "Mom may I have a snack from my Halloween snack bowl?" I agreed, so Jack ripped open a small snicker bar and quickly ate it. Through chocolaty teeth he said, "That snack wasn't strong enough, I need another one."

Jack, 3 – Florida

I asked my second grade class, "What are the four seasons?" One student raised his hand and answered, "Salt, Pepper, Mustard, Ketchup."

Second Grade Teacher – Ohio

I gave my daughter gum as a reward, though she tended to swallow it sometimes. One day while rewarding her for good behavior I warned "Savannah, do not swallow your gum or you won't get another piece." Two minutes later, I see she's not chewing the gum so I ask, "Did you swallow it?" With an innocent look on her face she replied, "No, I'm just holding it in my tummy."

Savannah, 3 – North Carolina

My friend's daughter, Isabella, was at the grocery store with her mom. As they passed the liquor section, Isabella pointed at the wine bottles and said loudly, "Look Mommy, there's your juice."

Isabella, 2 – New Jersey

I think I may have scarred my daughter Izzy, for life. Tonight I served her fish sticks for dinner and gave her a Finding Nemo fork to eat them with. Whoops.

Izzy, 8 – Tenessee

I was meeting my husband at California Pizza and running late. So when he called, I asked him to order for us. After surveying the kids for what they wanted, I received the usual requests – pasta, chips and salsa, ravioli. All was going well until I received my three year old's order. He asked for "A cheese pizza with spots."

Spencer, 3 – California

The other night we were eating ribs for dinner and my five year old said, "This is good pig on a cob."

Laurel, 5 – Michigan

This morning I was asked to go on a lunch date at the school cafeteria by my adorable little five year old. As I walked into the cafeteria, my son greeted me with a smile and tried to make me feel welcomed by saying "Mommy, the school lunches are so good. You're going to like it better than the food you cook. I know I do."

Eythen, 6 – Kansas

We were driving when we passed by five police cars in front of a house on our street. I said to my daughter "Look at all those police cars near our home." Unexpectedly she replied, "I guess Dunkin Donuts is empty tonight."

Emma, 8 – Michigan

Cathy, my sister, and Meranda, my niece, went to their favorite restaurant. Unfortunately for my sister, when you walk in the entrance there's a big bubble gum machine. Meranda was sitting in her buggy and said, "Mom, can I have a piece of gum?" Cathy replied, "Not yet, maybe on the way out." Meranda was persistent and continued to ask, driving Cathy to say, "Meranda, if you ask for a piece of gum again, we're going to leave now and you won't get a piece at all." Well, Meranda thought for a bit and then said "Mom, can I have a quarter?"

Meranda, 3 – Maine

We were all eating dinner, and there was a bottle of Hidden Valley ranch dressing on the table. I noticed my brother staring at the bottle intently. Finally he utters "You know one day I'll find the Hidden Valley ranch, and I'll share the secret with everyone I know."

Dewey, 4 – Montana

"I love to drink milk even if it is Cow pee pee," my daughter said at dinner. "It's not pee, its milk...just like when I breast fed you as a baby" I corrected her. "Gross. Can we just go with the cow pee pee instead?" my daughter pleaded.

Izzy, 6 – Tennessee

I took my niece to McDonalds. When it was time to order, the cashier asked her what she would like. Barely able to see over the counter, Tonya said, "I would like a hang burger and sick fries."

Tonya, 4 – Ohio

After sleeping over at her cousin's house, my daughter told her uncle, "I'll have ice cream for breakfast." He explained to her, "It's not part of a good diet, especially for breakfast." She assured him "That's Ok, I'm not on a diet."

Anonymous, 5 – Pennsylvania

My daughter begged of me "Please Daddy, I want something to eat...let's go to McDonald's." Unable to refuse her request, I drove to McDonalds. "Here's your Happy Meal. Are you happy now?" I said exasperated and expecting a little show of gratitude. "Yeah, until my Happy Meal wears off."

Anonymous, 8 – Illinois

My daughter innocently asked me the other day, "If chicken comes from a chicken, and turkey comes from a turkey...does pork come from a pork-u-pine?

Alyssa – Oregon

We were learning about nuts, so I said to my Pre-K class, "There are all kinds of nuts like peanuts, hazelnuts, and walnuts. What is your favorite nut?" A little boy immediately raised his hand and replied, "My favorite is the donut."

Pre-K Teacher - Pennsylvania

One evening when my nephew was visiting, we were about to eat dinner and I asked him if he wanted some broccoli. He replied, "No Auntie. I don't eat little trees."

HontheP.com

We were ordering dinner at a restaurant when my son told the waitress, "I would like the steak." The waitress asked, "How would you like it cooked honey – medium rare?" My son replied, "No, large rare please. I'm really hungry."

Liam, 10 – Utah

I was at the beach with my niece when she asked why the water tasted funny. I explained that ocean water is salt water. She looked out at the vast ocean and then asked, "Where did they get all the salt to put in there?"

Lia, 8 – Massachusetts

While grocery shopping, my son asked, "Can we get ice cream?" I told him "It's not on the list." Disappointed he asked "What about chips and salsa?" Once again I told him, "No, it's not on the list." Getting frustrated he asked "What about cookies?" Yet again I replied, "Sorry, it's not on the list." Fed up my son said "gotta' pen?"

Anonymous, 5 – North Carolina

My nephew Oliver and his friend Sam were having lunch. Noticing Oliver's mom was a little grouchy, Sam asked, "Isn't your mom having lunch, too?" "No, she is on a diet," said Oliver. Sam replied, "A diet? I would hate to be her. Without candy I would get mean." Oliver responded, "Tell me about it... I have to live with her."

Oliver, 7 - Ohio

POTTY TRAINING

My sister called me complaining that she had just changed the stinky diapers of her nine month and two year old...and needless to say she was done with poop for a while. Then she walked into the kitchen, where her six year old was eating lunch, and a whiff of poop went into her nostrils. In disbelief she said, "Who smells like poop now?" With a guilty look on her face, the six year old replied, "I don't know, but that smell has been following me all day."

Kelly-Rae, 6 – New York

We were in line buying a potty chair to toilet train my young son. He announced to the lady in line behind us, "I'm getting potty trained...then no more F**king diapers." We were way more careful about what we said around the kids after that.

Mikey, 3 – Texas

After coming out of the bathroom, my daughter asked curiously "Why do you spend so much time in the bathroom sometimes?" I replied honestly "I sit there and read." "I thought boys stand up when they go" she commented. "Not all the time" I said. After pausing for a moment she added, "If you sit on the potty, do you still have one of those things then, you know...a vigina stick?"

Anonymous, 4 – Ohio

After watching me change the sheets on our bed, my daughter asked. "Mommy, did you pee in your bed too?"

Delaney, 3 – Colorado
Peelinganorangewithascrewdriver.blogspot.com

When I started potty training my daughter, every time she would use the potty I would say "Good job, get yourself a candy. Then she'd run to get an M&M. One day, I was using the potty when she walked in on me and said, "Great job Mom, get yourself an M&M." So I did.

Mariah, 2 – Texas

I went to my daughter's room to wake her up one morning only to discover she was already awake. She told me, "Mommy, I couldn't sleep last night because of the pea." "You wet your bed?" I asked surprised because she hadn't done this in a long time. "I don't see any pee in it," I said. She replied, "No the pea is under my bed, like in the story, The Princess and the Pea."

Anonymous, 5 - North Carolina

We were potty training my youngest son, and things weren't going well. One night, as I was taking his diaper off and changing him into PJ's, Jack announced "I have to use the potty." My older kids and I watched in anticipation as he marched into the bathroom, flipped on the light, and scooted onto the potty backwards. Suddenly we hear Jack say "Abracadabra" followed by silence and then the beautiful sound of him whizzing into the potty. I guess the answer to potty training all came down to knowing the right magical word to say.

Jack, 2 – Nebraska

When my son potty trained at three, we promised him a new bike if he gave up diapers. He potty trained immediately and collected his reward with a smile. At four, he said "Mama, I'm thinking about potty training again." Surprised, I replied "But you're already potty trained." So he said "Well, how am I going to get a new bike then?"

Tommy, 3 – Oregon

One Sunday at church my son mentioned he had to use the little boy's room. I told him to go by himself and to meet us in the sanctuary when he was done. The church is so small, the bathrooms are right next to the sanctuary. My son was newly potty trained and neglected to tell me that he had to go number two. In the middle of prayers, a loud voice could be heard throughout the sanctuary shouting, "Mommy, come wipe my butt."

Roman, 3 – Nebraska

I had been struggling with potty training my daughter for a while. One day, I was standing over her waiting for her to pee in the big potty, and suddenly that blessed sound filled the small bathroom. She looked up at me with a big smile, and said, "It's music to your ears isn't it." And she was right.

Bethany, 2 – Pennsylvania
http://thegreengrandma.blogspot.com

In Pre-K most kids are newly potty trained, so we have to help the children to the bathroom a lot. It's not the most pleasant part of the job, but I could tolerate it except for one particular time when the little girl stood up after using the potty, looked in the toilet, and announced "That looks just like what we ate for dinner last night."

Anonymous, Pre-Kindergarten

After a day of skiing, I plopped my cold, marshmallow self onto the coach and said to my niece, "What a long day...Ella I am pooped." Ella, who had just become potty trained, replied, "You need to change your panties? That's OK...accidents happen."

Ella – Washington
Gianandmckinley.blogspot.com

At my son's Lacrosse game, my daughter needed to use the bathroom, but she refused to use the nearby port-a-potty. So I took her to a wooded area where she relieved herself. On the way back she observed, "Boys are lucky because their penies point out...girls aren't lucky because theirs point in, which means girls get pee on their flip flops."

Abby, 9 – Minnesota
www.joubiejou.com

RELIGION

While praying, my son, Dan, recently said, "Dear God, I bet it's very hard for you to love all the people in the world. There are only four people in our family, and I can't even do that."

Dan, 5 – Tennessee

"Honey, what are you doing?" I yelled as I surveyed the scene. Maroon nail polish was smeared all over my bedroom floor, complete with handprints on my white bathroom door that looked like a scene out of CSI Miami. "My painted toes are pretty Daddy don't you think?" Cadence replied beaming. Her toes were nearly glued together with congealing sludge. Still in shock I asked "But who said you could do this?" Without hesitating she answered, "God said it was OK."

Cadence, 3 – North Carolina

My friend was telling her husband she wanted a new car. Her husband told her it was too expensive and they couldn't afford it right now. Overhearing the conversation, their five year old piped up, "I know what to do, just ask for a car for Christmas. It's free if Santa brings it."

Brie, 5 – Virginia

After my seven year old caught wind of a certain "unsavory" fact about his eighteen-year-old cousin, he screamed in disbelief at him, "You don't believe in Santa? Well then Santa probably doesn't believe in you either."

Kurt, 7 – Vermont

Passing by our church, my daughter said to her friend, "See that church over there, that's where I was sanitized." (Baptized)

Mara, 5 – Massachusetts

When Noah was about three, he was really puzzled about Santa Claus. "I just don't understand," he said "How can the reindeer fly the sleigh? They don't even have a tank to put the gas in."

Noah, 3 – South Carolina

I have a nephew who has a habit of saying "Holy Cow" around his sister. At Sunday School one day, the teacher decided to quiz the students with a fill in the blank. One of the questions asked was "Who are the 3 spirits? The Father, the Son and the _____. And wouldn't you know it, my niece wrote "Holy Cow."

Anonymous, 3 – Texas

My three-year-old son recently asked my husband "How does Santa get in the house? My husband explained to him, "Down the chimney." Astonished my son said, "Well you should break his legs for breaking into the house...everyone else knocks at the door."

William, 3 – Georgia

During a recent drive, my wife and I told our three young children that God owned all the cattle on the miles of hills that were all around. A few seconds later as our six-year-old son looked out the car window he said, "And he owns that junky house on the hill that we just passed too?"

Issac, 6 – Hawaii

My son, Noah, has been asking questions about dating lately. My husband and I explained that you need to put a lot of prayer and thought into it in order to make a good choice. Noah pondered this and then quipped, "Well, I think I'll wait until after I get married to start dating then."

Noah, 6 – South Carolina

I was trying to get the last of the ketchup out of the bottle for my daughter's lunch, and it was quickly becoming a messy affair. That's when the phone rang, and my daughter answered it saying, "It's the Minister." With ketchup all over my hands I replied, "Tell him I can't come to the phone, and I'll call him back." That's when I heard my darling daughter say "Mommy can't come to the phone right now, she's hitting the bottle."

Anonymous, 4 – Kansas

While waiting for Daddy in the car, I popped a bible quiz on my kids. "In the bible, who defeated Goliath?" I tested my kids. Chaz replied "Luke Skywalker". Surprised I asked, "Why do you think that, Chaz?" "Because he's the legend of all legends. Who else would be able to defeat Goliath?" he reasoned.

Chaz, 10 – Arizona
Amazingsix.blogspot.com

This is my daughter's recent take on marriage: "No one really decides before they grow up whom they're going to marry. God decides it all way before...and you get to find out later who you're stuck with."

Kristin, 10 – Connecticut

One of my students came late to Sunday school class. He was usually very prompt, so I asked him if anything was wrong. He replied he had planned to go fishing, but his dad told him he needed to go to church instead. I was impressed and asked the boy if his father had explained why it was more important to go to church than to go fishing. To which the student replied, "Yes he did. My dad said that he didn't have enough bait for both of us."

Kyle, 8 – Michigan

My daughter told me her best friend wasn't in school because she had to do something with her community on Sunday and was too tired. Confused I asked "What community?" She replied, "You know the one where they wear all white and parade around." Hoping her friend wasn't part of the KKK I asked, "Do you mean communion?" She nodded "Oh yeah, that's it."

Victoria, 8 – Massachusetts

It had been raining hard all day, and my grandson commented that he was tired of the rain. "That's how God waters the flowers and trees," I informed him. With a serious look he replied, "But Grandma you need to tell God they have enough water 'cause I want to play outside."

Anonymous, 5 – North Carolina

One day my five-year-old daughter told me her mommy was taking her to her cousin's Bar Mitzvah out of state. I asked "Do you know what a Bar Mitzvah is?" She replied confidently, "Yes, it's something they do in New Jersey."

Anonymous, 5 – Maine

We recently had our second child, Matthew. Our three year old, Mikey, was so excited about his new baby brother that he often helped with feeding, diaper changes and even bath time. Well, last week Mikey took it upon himself to change a "stinky" diaper without my knowledge while I was busy washing dishes. The next thing I know, Mikey is standing behind me covered in Matthew's poop saying, "Being a Mommy is a dirty, stinky job isn't it?" When I nodded in agreement he said, "Thank you God for making me a boy so when I grow up I don't have to do the Mommy jobs."

Mikey, 3 – Pennsylvania

After looking at my baby pictures in black and white, my son asked, "Mom when did God invent color?"

David, 6 – Ohio

After church one Sunday morning on the ride home my son announced, "Mom, I've decided to become a Minister when I grow up." Not sure what to make of this new revelation since I didn't think my active son was the type to pursue such a calling, I responded, "That's okay, but what made you decide this?" He responded "Well, you make me go to church every Sunday anyway, so I figured it would be more fun to stand up and yell instead of having to sit and listen."

Stephen, 8 – Kansas

This is a conversation I overheard between my daughter and her friend. "What does baptize mean?" my daughter asked. Her friend replied, "I think baptism is when you get your sins washed out of your hair."

Addie, 6 – Michigan

We were talking about different religions at the dinner table and how they celebrate the holidays. Suddenly my son says, "There's a kid in my class, Jordan, and his Mom started out celebrating Christmas, but now his mom and Jordan celebrate Hanukah...you know I think they transferred to Jewish."

William, 9 – New Jersey

My daughter, Lani, asked "Dad where is God?" I replied confidently "God is everywhere and in all things." Not yet satisfied, Lani said, "Is God in the trees, the car and my silly bandz, too?" Exasperated I replied "Yes, yes and yes." Lani then took off one bracelet and began aggressively stretching it in all directions. She then asked "Does God mind when I do this to him?"

Lani, Michigan - 5

At Sunday school, I asked the students how God created the Earth. A student replied, "In the beginning which occurred near the start, there was nothing but God, darkness and some gas." Impressed I asked "And does the bible say anything else?" Thinking for a moment, the student replied, "The Bible also says the Lord thy God is one. But I happen to think he must be a lot older than that."

Anonymous, 8 – Kentucky

I told my son one evening to go to the back porch and bring me the broom. Frightened he said, "Mom, I'm afraid of the dark." I replied, "Don't be afraid, Jesus is everywhere, and he'll protect you." Still not convinced he said, "Are you sure he's out there?" Confidently I replied, "Yes, I'm sure and he's always ready to help when you ask him." Thinking for a moment, my son went to the back door, cracked it open and shouted into the darkness "Jesus, if you're really there please hand me the broom."

Anonymous – Maryland

Worried about my daughter getting reprimanded for talking too much, I asked her if she'd gotten in trouble yet for talking in school. She replied earnestly, "God gave me a mouth for talking, and I'm going to use it!"

Izzy, 6 – Tennessee

The Sunday school teacher instructed the kids "The Bible says that when Jesus was twelve, his parents dedicated him to God at church. That's when he became a man." One of the Sixth Graders raised his hand and added "I get it...they took him to God's house because his voice was changing, his armpits were getting smelly, and he was going to start plubery just like me."

Sixth Grade Teacher – Massachusetts

"What kind of church is that?" my son asked as we drove by. I told him it was a Catholic church. Pausing for a second he said, "I never want to go there...I might catch Catholic's foot."

Sonny, 7 – North Dakota

Our six-year-old daughter asked my husband "What does resurrection mean?" My husband explained to her "Resurrection means that Jesus came back to life after death." With a look of bewilderment she said, "Like a zombie?"

Katie, 6 – Michigan

I was shopping with my son when he turned to me and said, "If God is everywhere, why isn't he at Walmart when I tell him I need toys?" Not knowing how to respond I simply said, "I don't know." So he continued, "At church they say God gives us what we need, and I need him to pass my messages onto you."

Josiah, 7 – Pennsylvania

One of my first grade students had to leave, so I asked him "Why are you leaving early?" He proudly told me, "I'm having my baby brother donated today." (Dedicated)

Kindergarten Teacher – Kentucky

HALL OF FAME

Since it was around Christmas time, and I teach Sunday school, I decided to ask the class "Where is Jesus today?" Steven raised his hand and said, "He's in heaven." Sarah called out "He's in my heart." And then out of nowhere Michael blurted, "I know...he's in our bathroom." The whole class got very quiet, and I was at a loss for words until I asked, "Why did you say that?" Michael replied "Because I hear my Father get up in the morning, bang on the bathroom door and yell, "Good lord, are you still in there?"

Michael, 4 – Pennsylvania

My son became very curious as to how Santa found us each year since we've moved three times in the past four years. So I made up a long, magical story about "How Santa's elves make special dust made of rainbows and candy canes that help the reindeer navigate to our new house." After finishing my exhaustively elaborate tale, my son simply responded, "Mom, wouldn't it be easier if he just used OnStar?"

Dylan, 7 – Georgia
Princessmuffintop.blogspot.com

The day after Christmas, my three-year-old son asked, "Mom is Santa going to die?" I told him I didn't think so. Still not reassured he said "Well I hope he doesn't die before next year because I need more Geotrax."

Anonymous, 3 – New Hampshire

I was babysitting Bri and reading her a Christmas story. I pointed out that Joseph was Jesus' stepfather, but that God was Jesus' real father. Bri, whose parents are divorced, thought this over for a moment then asked "Does Jesus see God on the weekends?"

Bri, 8 – Michigan

I recently asked my three year old to "Give me a moment of quiet." In all seriousness he looked at me and said, "Mommy, my mouth doesn't do quiet."

Anonymous, 3 – Massachusetts

A Mom at school was chatting about how her neighbors are expecting their first baby. I laughed thinking what those neighbors don't know. After my first was born, it wasn't long before I found myself uttering phrases I never imagined. My top 10 are:

1. You can't just pee on anyone's car, only pee on our car
2. Pennies don't go in the CD player; it's not a bank
3. No it's not OK to touch his penis
4. Don't drink the mustard
5. The computer mouse is not a racecar, give it back
6. The violin is not a guitar
7. Underwear is not optional, it's necessary
8. "Goodest" is not a word
9. That's not the neighbor's sandbox, it's kitty litter
10. Yes all the mannequins have boobies, now put her shirt down

4Kids, – Pennsylvania
www.hillsnapshot.blogspot.com

While teaching an art class, I told the students to draw anything they'd like in class that day. This of course met with a lot of cheers and excitement. As I walked around the classroom looking at the student's beautiful drawings of pirates, spaceships, flowers and rainbows, I was struck by the lack of a drawing by one of my best students, Sally. "What are you drawing?" I asked concerned. Sally replied, "I'm going to draw God." Trying to make Sally feel better I said, "Well honey, no one really knows what God looks like." Sally smiled at me confidently and replied, "Well they will in a minute."

Sally, 8 – Indiana

My son wrote the following message to his soccer coach on his holiday card. "It's okay that you yell. My dad yells sometimes, and he says he wouldn't do it if he didn't care. You must care a lot."

Max, 11 – Michigan

On the first day of first grade, a little boy came up to me at noon and asked, "Where's my mom? I'm ready to go home." I explained to him, "Last year was Kindergarten, and you went half days, but in first grade you stay a full day." Speechless, he looked then replied "Who the hell signed me up for that?"

1st Grade Teacher – Pennsylvania

One Sunday after church, my daughter asked me if she could go outside to play with the boys. I told her "No, you can't play with the boys, they're too rough." My daughter thought about it for a moment and then said, "If I can find a smooth one, can I play with him?"

Anonymous, 7 – Pennsylvania

I overheard this conversation between my fourteen-year-old daughter and her younger brother: "I'm having problems with my computer," my son said. My daughter replied "Stop complaining, you're so lucky, when I was your age all we had was dial up."

Kendra, 14 – Michigan

On the first day of day care, the teacher asked JC to tell the class a little about himself. JC was ready for this question since his sister was five and had already taught him the ropes. So JC stood up and said with confidence "I have a dog named Jasper, I like to ride in the boat and go to the beach, my sister is in the class across the hall, my daddy owns a business and my mama is a prostitute." On JC's second day he had added a new phrase to his vocabulary "District Attorney."

John, 4 – California

I overheard one of my first grade students telling his mom one day "First Grade is so tough, I think it can only be handled by Second Graders."

1st Grade Teacher – California

When the erupting volcano was all over the news in 1980, my son came rushing into the room and yelled excitedly, "Dad, Mt. St. Helens is interrupting."

Liam, 7 – Oregon

A while ago my son and I were talking about the war in Iraq. I was telling him about 9/11 and how Osama Bin Laden was the bad guy we were looking for. He asked, "Why can't they just find him?" I answered honestly "I don't know." Shaking his head he replied "I get it, there must be too many Laden's in the phone book."

Anonymous, 5 – North Carolina

On the first day of day care, the teacher asked JC to tell the class a little about himself. JC was ready for this question since his sister was five and had already taught him the ropes. So JC stood up and said with confidence "I have a dog named Jasper, I like to ride in the boat and go to the beach, m sister is in the class across the hall, my daddy owns a business and my mommy is a prostitute." On JC's second day, he added a new phrase to his vocabulary, "District Attorney."

John, 4 – California

I overheard one of my first grade students telling his mom one day "First grade is so tough, I think it can only be handled by second graders."

1st Grade Teacher – Indiana

My daughter and her classmates each drew names of famous historical figures to research and debate. My daughter drew Marco Polo and won her first debate against Genghis Kahn. Next she debated Ghandi and won. She continued to win until her last debate. When I asked why she thought she lost, my daughter said honestly "Well it's hard to win a debate against Jesus."

Madison, 12 – Arizona

After purchasing a warranty for his truck, my husband was extremely upset when it broke down and the broken part wasn't covered. Frustrated he yelled "Lifetime warranty my a**." Our son overheard this and asked "Dad what's a lifetime warranty?" "It means you get screwed" my husband replied still upset. My son who was always getting into trouble and was no stranger to time outs said, "Well I guess I get lifetime warranties all the time."

Anonymous, 5 – West Virginia

When my dad passed away, we had to dispose of some of his things including his various collections of unrelated stuff. My daughter, who was 11 at the time, was helping us. During the process she came upon a rather large bottle of assorted marbles. My daughter took one look at them and said unexpectedly, "At least Grandpa didn't lose all his marbles before he died."

Anonymous, 11 – California

"Oh sugar," a Pre-K student said in Sunday school. I asked him, "Now why did you say that?" Looking at me like I should know, he replied, "Because I can't say sh*t in Sunday school."

Sunday School Teacher – Delaware

New to the neighborhood a little girl asked my daughter "What school do you go to?" My daughter replied, "I go to Catholic school because I'm Catholic." Then she asked the little girl, "And what school do you go to?" The little girl responded, "I go to public school, so I must be public."

Anonymous, 8 – Virginia

Black skirt that my daughter will wear exactly one time for her band concert: $25. Bribe that I had to pay to get her to wear the skirt: $7. Consenting to let her wear leggings under the skirt and avoiding what would have been a Basic Instinct moment...priceless.

Molly, 9 – Michigan

I told my kids that when I was little, we didn't have any computers. Astounded my daughter replied, "That's impossible, how did you check your e-mail?"

Anonymous, 6 – New York

 While at the beach, my son ran out of the water yelling "I've been stung by a jellyfish." My husband immediately asked, "How do you know?" My son screamed, "Because it had giant testicles."

Anonymous, 11 – Florida

We were watching the basketball playoffs on TV with our nephew, Connor, when he asked, "Uncle Brian why aren't they playing?" I replied, "Because the coach called a time out." Connor asked, "What did they get in trouble for?"

Connor, 4 – California

To keep my son busy while I cleaned the kitchen, I told him to draw what he saw on TV. I was shocked when I checked on him and found he had followed my directions to the letter. The entire surface of the TV screen was colored in crayon.

Billy , 4 - New York

This was as sincere and remorseful as my daughter could get as she wrote an apology note to her three brothers for the mistreatment they suffered from her. "I'm sorry for all the mean things I said to you this year, and the way meaner things I thought about you."

Molly, 9 – Michigan

We were going to a nicer-than-usual-restaurant with our three kids when my six-year-old son announced he was going to "dress up." Impressed we waited and tried not to laugh when he showed up in his Halloween costume dressed as a cowboy. The next thing I knew, my daughter ran to change into her cheerleading costume so she could be "dressed up" too. We finally left, and I thought things were going relatively well with three young kids in a restaurant, that was until my daughter crossed her legs, and I realized she was missing one important article of clothing.

Victoria, 3 – New Jersey

My nine-year-old son was slightly annoyed that I was cleaning the family room while he watched TV. "I don't understand why you can't just sit down and relax" he commented. "Well I've got to clean up this mess. Unfortunately a messy house can't clean itself" I answered. After thinking for a moment, my son replied, "Well, unfortunately for me, the TV can't watch itself either."

Thomas, 9 – New York

My husband and I left our son, Ben, in the care of his Aunt to go on our first vacation without him. Knowing he would have a hard time sleeping while we were gone, Ben's Aunt said, "Now that Mom and Dad went on a trip, you're going to have to be brave and sleep all by yourself. Clearly upset, my son replied, "But Daddy isn't brave…he always sleeps with Mommy."

Ben, 5 – South Carolina

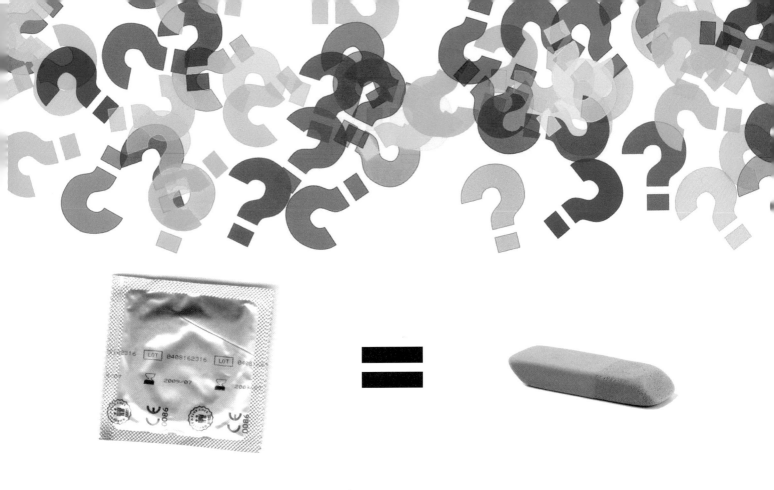

When new First Grader from Scotland raised his hand and said, "Teacher, may I have a rubber?" the teacher was shocked and sent him to the principal's office. When the school phoned his mother, she said that she couldn't understand why the teacher didn't have rubbers to pass out to all the students. After further discussion, it came to light that in Scotland, a rubber is an eraser.

Anonymous, 7 - Pennsylvania

BIRDS & BEES

My daughter is the youngest of four children, so I had some experience giving the "Sex Talk." When it came time to have "The Talk", I thought I did a great job of sitting her down and explaining all the details about having sex and making a baby...that was until she said with a horrified look on her face "You mean you did that four times?"

Marla, 11 – Kentucky

I needed a new couch so I took my daughter furniture shopping with me. We looked at many couches, and I had to decide between a large sectional couch and a smaller sofa. I chose the smaller sofa which was delivered a week later. My daughter took one look at it and said "Mom I really wish you would have bought that sexual couch instead...I liked it much better."

Anonymous, 7 – North Carolina

The only thing worse than having "The Sex Talk" with your child is discovering your twelve year old has already given "The Talk" to her younger sister. "Why did you do that?" I asked my older daughter, Hannah. "Well Bella's friends were passing along the wrong information...so I performed a public service." "What did you tell her?" I asked tentatively. "I told her when you find a boy you like you should have sex with him...in a bedroom, or in a car, or in the back bathroom of a bar." Let this be a warning to other parents never let your older child give the "Sex Talk" to your younger one.

Hannah, 12 – Michigan

My daughter, Harleigh, asked, "Mommy, how do animals get the babies out of their tummies? Not ready for the birds and the bees' talk, I lied and said, "I'm not sure. Refusing to give up, Harliegh said, "Maybe Daddy knows?" I replied, "I am pretty sure Daddy has no idea where babies come from." Harleigh nodded, "I guess that makes sense since Mommies know everything and Daddies work hard." My son overheard our conversation and decided to defend the male race by saying, "I know where they come from...Babies come out of your butt. Where else could they come out?"

Ethyne, 6 – Kansas
Moorepartyof5.blogspot.com

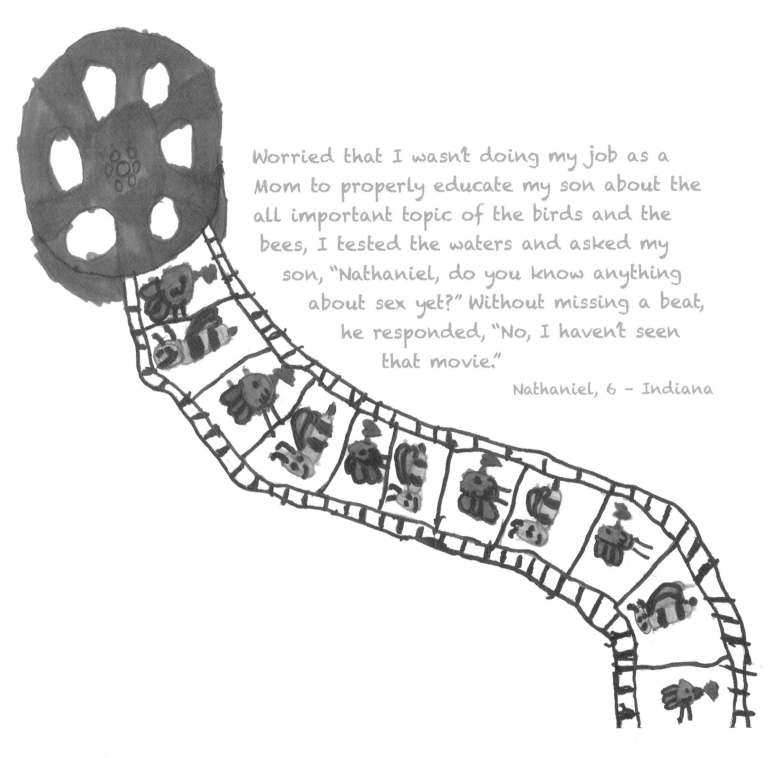

Worried that I wasn't doing my job as a Mom to properly educate my son about the all important topic of the birds and the bees, I tested the waters and asked my son, "Nathaniel, do you know anything about sex yet?" Without missing a beat, he responded, "No, I haven't seen that movie."

Nathaniel, 6 – Indiana

My older daughter was at that age where you have "The Talk." My sister is a biologist so I approached this as scientifically as I could. Our "Talk" must have really made an impression because later that night my daughter, a little hungry, came into the kitchen and asked, "Mom, can I eat some vagina sausages?" Now I will never be able to look at a Vienna sausage the same way again.

Anonymous, 5 – Colorado

When I started playing a board game with my youngest daughter, I said, "I don't remember how to play Operation." She reassured me by saying "Don't worry...we can just look at the erections and figure it out.

Madison, 5 – Wisconsin

Tony was staying at his grandmother's for a few days. He'd been playing outside with some neighborhood kids for awhile when he came into the house and asked "Grandma, what's that called when two people sleep in the same room and one is on top of the other?" Grandma was a little taken aback but decided to tell the truth and said, "It's called sexual intercourse." Tony replied, "OK" and went back outside to play with the other kids. A few minutes later, he came back in and said angrily "Grandma, it isn't called sexual intercourse. It's called bunk beds...and Jimmy's mom wants to talk to you."

Tony, 9 – Georgia

My granddaughter came home all excited and announced "We learned how to make babies in school today." "How?" I asked. "It's real simple," she replied, "You change the Y to I and add ES."

Billy, 6 – Louisiana

I picked my son up from his new school. He was so excited to tell me about his day and the first thing out of his mouth was "Mommy we have a kitchen center and it has hookers."

Nolan, 4- Texas

One day my daughter asked, "How did I get here?" Not wanting to go into detail, I responded, "We took a little bit of love from me and your father, mixed it all up, and got you." After pondering this for a moment, she asked, "Did you add milk?"

Lani, 5 - Michigan

I was driving my children, niece and their cousins to our house, the conversation turned to scary movies. My son told his cousins that he couldn't see PG-13 movies. My nephew informed him that "there are R rated movies that are even worse, and you have to be a parent to see them." My nephew added that there are even X rated movies. I grew concerned until he explained, "You have to be Grandma and Grandpa's age to see rated X movies because they're for old people."

Timothy, 8 – Vermont

I returned home from playing tennis with the neighbor on a particularly hot day. I told my daughter, Emily, to answer the phone if it rang, explaining I was going to take a quick shower to wash off the sweat. Of course the phone rang. It was my mother-in-law. I later found out Emily told her the following: "Sorry Mommy can't come to the phone right now. She was playing with the neighbor and got all hot and sweaty. So now she's taking a shower."

Emily, 6 – Ohio

Kaytlin's Mom was expecting a baby, which led to Kaytlin asking the inevitable "Where do babies come from?" After a short conversation, Kaytlin seemed appeased and went on her way. Later that evening Kaytlin and her daddy were wrestling when he playfully stepped on her stomach. Kaytlin sat straight up and shrieked, "Daddy, stop it. You're cracking my eggs."

Kaytlin, 5 – Connecticut

"Where do babies come from?" my son asked. Not wanting to deal with this question in detail at such a young age, I replied, "They come from the bottom of a woman's body." I was satisfied I'd handled the situation perfectly until my son said, "You mean I came from your toe?"

Jason, 5 – North Carolina

I was at the grocery store when out of the blue my son started yelling, "I want some sex." I tried to quiet him down, but he kept talking about sex and how much he liked it. I hurried out of the store and confronted my husband when I returned home, thinking he told our young son to say this as a joke. My husband immediately understood our son was asking for his favorite snack—Chex.

Dax – Washington

Blog Contributors

ADOPTION AND FERTILITY

Amothershood.com

Adoption/Breast Cancer/Family

I love taking care of my family. I used to fight the title of stay-at-home mom - I'm much more than that. I'm a lawyer and businesswoman, cancer survivor, and I was a widow. Now I have two adopted daughters and I'm married to a Texan who is truly my better half. I have a lot to blog about.

Bridgetobaby.com

Infertility/Parenting/Pregnancy

Bridging is a way of connecting people so they can share their experiences about infertility and pregnancy. Once you open up and share, others will feel inclined to so the same.

ADVICE

Grammyslists.com

Advice/Activities/Recipes

This blog is all things for and about grandkids. I'm Grammy to three beautiful girls. I create activities that are both educational and fun for grandkids. I invite you to use and share the ideas you find to make Grammy's or Mommy's journey a little easier and more fun.

Mommycribnotes.com

Advice/Humor/Parenting

I'm a crazed Mom of two kids 18 months apart. One was planned and the other, not so much. I'll do chocolate, caffeine, and Gregorian chants to maintain inner peace. I'm striving for a balance, but making do with a multi-tasking juggling act. I started this blog to give other Moms a "cheat sheet" of discoveries, tips, and gadgets that will make parenting easier.

Mommyspen.com

Advice/Diabetes/Freelancing

When I came home from the hospital after having my daughter, I knew I would write. I always wanted to be a writer, but excuses were easy to make. Having a kid lit a fire under me. I'm modeling an attitude I want for my daughter. I'm also a business systems analyst, freelance writer, gardener, knitter, spinner, and chicken-keeper.

www.Ponderingjane.com

Advice/Attachment Parenting/Family

Pondering Jane is a place that offers real and practical support to families, specifically those with a stay-at-home parent and those practicing Attachment Parenting. The hope is that by offering resources and real accounts of day-to-day parenting struggles, visitors will understand that they're not alone and will have resources available to better handle difficult situations.

Theadventureofsupermom.com

Advice/Gardening/Recipes

As a mother of four children ranging in age from a teenager to a toddler, I deal with a lot of things most Moms relate to like teenager behavior, potty training, saving money, etc. I tell funny stories and give helpful advice.

What-mama-wants.com

Green Living/Recipes/Reviews

I love to support quality products and companies. What Mama Wants is a blog for parents who are interested in reviews, giveaways, cloth diapering, breastfeeding, green living, healthy cooking, and just plain family fun. My mission is to bring quality companies and product to the parents who use them.

ASPERGER AND AUTISM

Amazingsix.blogspot.com

Asperger/Health/Homeschooling

I'm 32 years old and the mother of six – four boys and two girls. We also have a huge Great Dane and chickens. I enjoy my vegetable garden, homeschooling, and being a stay-at-home mom. I wouldn't have it any other way.

Blog.mamasturnnow.com

Asperger/Autism

I love being a Mom, but sometimes it just isn't enough - especially if you're a Mom of a child with Asperger's, another with severe asthma, and a husband who travels a lot for work. Yet I'm determined to take this journey. My hope is that through my odyssey you will be encouraged to start your own.

Fourplusanangel.com

Autism/Loss/Triplets

I'm Mom to five children, four in my arms and one in my heart. My life is full of ups and downs. I began motherhood as a teen parent with a daughter who has autism. I went on to meet my husband, and after years of infertility, I had triplets only to lose one—a beautiful daughter. A year later, we found out we were pregnant with my youngest, our rainbow baby.

Joubiejou.com

Asperger/Joubert Syndrome

This blog is written about my family. We have two children with a rare genetic disorder called Joubert Syndrome and a boy with Asperger's Syndrome.

Theconnorchronicles.wordpress.com

Autism/Asperger/Humor

This blog chronicles our family's adventure raising a child with ADHD and Asperger's.

BOOK REVIEWS

Marshmallowmondays.wordpress.com

Book Reviews/Family

I live in Pennsylvania with my husband, six-year-old son, a new baby and our cat and dog. Between the kids and the pets, life is always entertaining and delightfully rewarding. I don't believe in regrets. I do believe that life prepares you for every big chapter that comes your way. The past is simply the groundwork for the future.

Whisperswhispering.blogspot.com

Activities/Book Reviews/Homeschooling

I'm a Grandma to a four year old. Parenting the second time around has been wonderful. I share our homeschooling, play, and not so good experiences.

CRAFTS

Mommymayhemsurvivalguide.blogspot.com

Activities/Advice/Recipes

I'm a writer and Mommy from New York who started a blog to help other mothers. This is a place to find and share quick fixes on everything from diaper rash to dinner recipes. As a Mom, I understand the value of time and simplicity, so all of my posts are short and sweet.

Nomies3monsters.soopsee.com

Advice/Crafts/Pregnancy

I'm a 26-year-old stay-at-home mom to three monsters. I'm on my way to becoming a semi-crunchy Mommy despite what my Hubby says. I'm creating my niche in the blogging world with my unique observations.

www.Theknitwitbyshair.com

Advice/Book Reviews/Product Reviews

My blog is about my life as a happily married Mom to three young boys. It chronicles our life's journey, my hobbies, and obsessions. I also highlight products and giveaways from companies.

Thetrendytreehouse.blogspot.com

Crafts/Recipes/Tutorials

The Trendy Treehouse is a great place to find crafts, art projects, tutorials, recipes, reviews, giveaways, and more.

FAMILY

Aggraygate.blogspot.com

Photography/Recipes/Reviews

I'm a Writer, Artist, Wife, Mother, and Adventurer. This is my aggregate. My blog is a collection of my thoughts and experiences as I work towards creating the life I want to live and the woman I know I can be.

Biddlebuzz.com

Army/Family/Friends

We put this blog together to keep friends and family updated on our lives since we moved so far from everyone. There's always something entertaining happening, and I hope you find it interesting too.

Binkertation.com

Grad School/Pregnancy/Recipes

I'm a working Mom in my mid-twenties. I have the best husband in the world and an energetic three year old. To make things even more exciting, we're expecting a baby boy. I'm a full time grad student who has a hard time doing nothing. I'm working on slowing down to enjoy each moment a little more.

Gianandmckinley.blogspot.com

Family/Friends/Photos

I met my husband on a blind date and now we're expecting a baby, which means we're putting the plans to adopt a dog on hold for now. We're nothing out of the ordinary except for the fact that we appreciate a little spice in our life. I hope you find joy and humor throughout my blog.

Happytogetherish.blogspot.com

Family/Photos

This blog is about the misadventures and craziness of life. I'm a Mom to four kids. I didn't intend for my life to end up this way, but I'm really content. It was one heck of a journey, and I made a lot of mistakes that I'm still learning from. I'm raising my children in a loving, accepting, and judgment free home. I'm also learning about myself since through the years my "self" got lost.

Linsey-organizedchaos.blogspot.com

Family/Photography

I'm a wife to the love of my life and a Mom to four amazing kids. Life is full, and I love it. Living in the Rocky Mountains is so beautiful, I never want to leave. I have a camera, which I use a lot so you'll see lots of photos on my blog.

Littlestorieseverywhere.com

Commentary/Current Events

This blogging Mama writes about adventures in life, love, and laughter. Lighten up with little stories. They are everywhere after all.

Magpiemusing.com

Recipes/Crafts/Music

It's a journal, a scrapbook, a record of my kid's childhood. It's about food and the pleasures of gardening. It's about my one irascible child. It's where I wear my heart on my sleeve, play with words and rail at the world.

Onesiemommy.com

Books/Family/Only Children

I'm a Mother of one. I'm a Wife who thinks marriage and being a Teacher are more challenging now that I'm a Mother. I'm a woman who likes to look good and find time for herself while still trying to be a wonderful Mother. I created this blog to connect with other Moms of only children. I'm trying to find a balance between motherhood and everything else in life.

www.Oursweetstory.com

Advice/Family/Photography

This is the story of my sweet family, sweet dreams, and sweet life. Time is flying by so fast; I'm trying my best to soak up every sweet second. Whether it's capturing these moments with my camera or dreaming up big dreams, I hope to keep track of it all here.

Penelopeblue.blogspot.com

Family/Photography

This blog is about family life. The life I live with my husband, daughter, and two dogs.

Princessmuffintop.blogspot.com

Family/Commentary/Opinions

I support mediocrity hardcore. My blog is a commentary about life.

Ruminatingmommy.blogspot.com

Family/Fashion/Reviews

I have always loved writing and I hope others can connect with what I have to say. My aim is to be open and honest, and even witty from time to time. I'm a stay-at-home mom with one daughter, a husband, and a cat. I love fashion and my background is wedding design.

Sixcherriesontop.com

Army/Gardening/Photography

I was married to an abusive man with whom I had three daughters. He was a college grad with a promising future, and a few bad life choices changed it all. Drugs can truly undo a person and destroy relationships. I'm thankful I've been given a second chance at love. I've never been happier now that I'm married to my Marine with whom I have three boys now.

Texasmacks.blogspot.com

Photography/Recipes/Scrapbooking

My blog started out as a way to keep family and friends updated and to document the boys' growth. Now it's become a hobby and obsession. It's my therapy some days, other days it's my brag book. As a teacher, full-time wife and mother, it's a constant juggling act trying to manage it all. However, I wouldn't have it any other way.

FOOD

Stacymakescents.com

Coupons/Parenting/Recipes

I have several titles: Wife, Mommy, Cook, Baker, and Housekeeper. If you would have told me ten years ago I'd find myself in these shoes, I would have laughed. However, I'm very content in my life and where I've come from. I have a passion for finding good deals, eating healthy, and photography. I know the journey is only going to get better.

Thefootballwife.com

Football/Motherhood/Recipes

Life married to a college football coach is always full of surprises, and not just on game day. I'm the Football Wife. On my blog, you'll find my daily thoughts, inspirational recipes (especially for feeding a team), and how I keep myself busy during recruiting season (which usually involves redecorating something).

Yourworldnatural.blogspot.com

Health/Nutrition/Weight Loss

This blog is here to share the gift of good health and natural living so you can live your best life. You will find exciting giveaways and great products that have been reviewed by me.

HOMESCHOOL

Whisperswhispering.blogspot.com

Activities/Book Reviews/Homeschooling

I'm a grandma to a four year old. Parenting the second time around has been wonderful. I share the homeschooling, playtime, good and not so good experiences.

HUMOR

Justliketheanimal.blogspot.com

Humor/Parenting/Weight Loss

I'm a Mommy Blogger, wife, entrepreneur and done deaf rock star in the car. My other distinctions are that I'm a forgetful friend, directionally challenged, keeper of the dog treats. Read my blog and be entertained.

Laugh-quotes.com

Family/Humor

I'm a hilarious writer, brilliant graphic artist and talented travel photographer in my dreams. In real life, I'm just a Blogger writing about the day-to-day adventures that remind me that my life is a bit of a joke. I'm an American expat living and loving life in New Zealand.

Moorepartyof5.blogspot.com

Family/Humor/Photos

What can I say about the Moore household? How can you put so many wonderful feelings about your family into a word or phrase? The only way I can express how I feel about my life, kids and husband is... perfectly blessed.

Nixclips.blogspot.com

Family/Food/Humor

I'm a former teacher working as a freelance writer while attending graduate school. I blog about how we can blame our children for gray hairs and laugh lines in addition to sleepless nights and early mornings. In our house, we have crushed crackers in our couch, sticky door knobs, and sparkle bubble berry toothpaste smears on the bathroom counter. Welcome to my house, my life, and my family.

Peelinganorangewithascrewdriver.blogspot.com

Art/Depression/Humor

I'm a stay-at-home mom of three young children. My blog is where I go to ponder life in general. Things like parenting and marriage, diaper rash, dealing with depression, the angst of writer's block, and the freedom of a good book. Sometimes I even throw in a photo or poem.

Therealmattdaddy.com

Humor/Parenting/Reviews

I left my job as a manager for a national retail chain to be a stay-at-home dad for my little girl. Follow me as I attempt to laugh my way through the crying.

Timetomakethebrownies.wordpress.com

Guilt/Humor/Parenting

I love being a Mother, but no one is truly prepared for the chaos, uncertainty, and chronic fatigue that regularly define your days. To survive and enjoy the process, you've got to find the funny, embrace the numerous dysfunctional moments, and give yourself permission to be less than perfect. If something makes you laugh, cry, or irritates the hell out of you, I want to hear about it.

PRODUCTS

HeardonthePlayground.com

T-shirts

Custom t-shirts with limited edition funny kid sayings you won't find anywhere else. The t-shirts are unique and come in a variety of colors. Share the laughs and order your HeardonthePlayground t-shirt.

IStartus.com

Logo Design/SEO/Web Design

We're one of the leading web technology companies in the United States. We do search engine optimization, custom website development, logo design, custom code, and provide virtual web developers. We do it all.

Kreationz4kidz.com

Decorating/Wall Decals

This is where you'll find custom decals to decorate any kid's room. All our decals are created using a very professional, water resistant, matte finish, removable vinyl. You simply peel off the back coating and smooth it onto your desired location. When you're done with the decals, just peel them off. Custom orders are always welcome.

Spinningyarnspress.com

Coffee Table Books/Family Portraits/Senior Portraits

Many people know Robin for her unique coffee table books featuring original photography, poetry, and design. Her work spans the nation from Detroit to Florida and from California to New York. Robin Arm Photography also offers custom framed fine art wall portraits, jewelry, holiday cards, birth announcements, albums, image boxes, and more.

PRODUCT REVIEWS

Couponsoncaffeine.com

Humor/Savings/Single Mom

I'm a single Mom trying to stretch a buck while raising two boys. I'm a full time college student and a jack-of-all-trades.

Familyfocusblog.com

Activities/Green Living/Product Reviews

This blog is focused on going green and fun family activities. It's written by a stay-at-home mom blogger from Tennessee. I write about family fun, eco tips, giveaways, products and causes that you may find helpful or interesting.

Familylifeinlv.com

Family/Parenting/Product Reviews

My blog is about an East Coast born, mid western raised girl who followed her heart West. I'm a wife to an amazing man, and we have one boy. I'm a baby wearing, cloth diapering, going organic, extended breastfeeding, sleep deprived, stay-at-home mom who is learning the ropes as I go. All this while trying to figure out how to raise a family in Sin City.

Freebiesandmuchmore.com

Family/Product Reviews/Saving Money

This is a one-stop website full of family friendly ways to save money. The website is updated daily and includes free samples, money saving coupons, product giveaways, product testing opportunities, and much more.

Happeningsoftheharperhousehold.net

Green Living/Parenting/Product Reviews

This is a stay-at-home mommy blog about life with two little girls and a hubby who works the swing shift in the steel industry. I believe in cloth diapers, breast feeding, baby wearing, and co-sleeping. You can find a little of everything, and there's always one or two giveaways going on.

Mamaluvsbaby.com

Baby Products/Product Reviews

My blog was designed for new Moms to give them a sense of security, efficiency, and mobility. It's a one-stop shop for mommy and baby. I offer award-winning products that are hard to find. These products are chosen to make Mommy and baby happy and healthy. The majority of items offered are made by Moms.

Mommyhastowork.com

Green Living/Product Reviews/Saving Money

My blog is about going green, saving money, composting, life with kids, and product reviews.

Mommysmemorandum.com

Advice/Product Reviews/Recipes

I'm a 40 something stay-at-home mom to six amazing and active children. In 2007, I left my career in sales and middle management to pursue the career I've most coveted – being a Mommy. It was a life changing decision, and I have yet to look back with regret. My passion is writing.

Neworkingwitches.com

Coupons/Product Reviews/Saving Money

My blog is mainly about product reviews, giveaways, and saving money. I work to help other Moms save money and find products that are just right for their household.

Obviously-marvelous.com

Bargain Shopping/Family/Product Reviews

I'm born and raised in Las Vegas, Nevada. I'm a wife to my best friend. I have a college degree and am a licensed Cosmetologist, but I now have the best title ever - stay-at-home mom to my three amazing kids. I'm a loud, funny, outspoken, tattooed, atheist, bargain shopping, sports loving, giveaway fanatic who obviously has a lot to say.

Onemamasdailydrama.com

Coupons/Food/Product Reviews

I blog about shopping, coupons and deals. I like to share photos of my garden and funny personal stories as well. My life is a juggling act where I try to find balance between all the elements that make me who I am. If you can relate, I hope you'll join me on this crazy journey I call life.

Pays2save.com

Coupons/Product Reviews/Spiritual

I'm a Christian, wife, Mother, businesswoman, and student. I was in the Air Force and worked as a Licensed Practical Nurse before I got out. Now, I'm a stay-at-home mom with a family, quilting business, and a frugal blog. My motto is "Don't waste another dollar." I help others save by posting deals, coupons, free samples, and much more.

Realmomreviews.net

Coupons/Family/Product Reviews

I'm a Mom to six kids. As you can imagine, I have a lot to blog about.

Spoiledbutnotrotten.net

Coupons/Deals/Product Reviews

This blog is dedicated to helping parents find deals on stuff for kids of all ages. Find the best deals on baby gear, diapers, clothes, toys, and much more.

Thegreengrandma.blogspot.com

Green Living/Product Reviews

This blog is where old-fashioned ways combine with 21st century common sense. Let's show the next generation we care by making small sacrifices here and there to ensure a better future for all. Let's help each other to lead healthier lives – physically, emotionally, and spiritually.

Thenightowlmama.com

Family/Product Reviews/Videos

We're a family of six sharing our daily lives and experiences with products, posts, and videos. If you wish to have a product reviewed or advertised, I'd love to hear from you.

SPIRITUALITY

Kristyblogs.com

Family/Religion

My blog documents my journey through marriage, motherhood, and finding out what it truly means to be a woman of God. I'd love for you to join me.

Mommyventures.wordpress.com

Family/Religion

I'm starting this blog with a new outlook on motherhood. I have four children under eight. I'm always looking for tips, tricks, and Moms like me. I hope this blog helps jog my memory when looking back at my life and also helps other Moms as well. I'm looking to make friends out of this and connect with other mommies that have more than the average family.

TWINS

3in2.blogspot.com

Identical Twins/Pregnancy/Parenting

My blog is about going from zero to three kids in 16 months: one son in March 2010 and identical twin daughters.

Lilbumpkin.blogspot.com

Family/Humor/Twins

This blog is a journey through marriage, a miscarriage, and the miracle of twins.

TRAVEL

Hillsnapshot.blogspot.com

Family/Photography/Travel

Snippets and snapshots of today's moments and tomorrow's memories. A family of four with two furry friends travels the world.

About the Author

I have a very talented family. My ten-year-old can make his butt "talk." My seven-year-old believes glue guns are a right not a privilege. And my three-year-old is training to be a dictator by refusing to acknowledge the word "No." Being blessed with so many characters in one family means that each day is more entertaining than the next. Hoping I wasn't the only parent to give birth to The Little Rascals instead of the Brady Bunch, I started a website to collect funny kid stories,

HeardonthePlayground.com. I was immediately overwhelmed by the response as shocking, embarrassing and hysterical stories about kids poured in from across the nation. I never thought topics such as peeing, nose picking, sex, and even death could be so funny. I'm not just a Midwestern Mom of three with two graduate degrees I never use with one husband who was convinced his children are destined to be circus performers. Now I am a woman with peace of mind who can look her husband in the eyes with complete honesty and say "Hey, lots of kids are like that…"

Share the laughs....

If you have a funny, shocking or entertaining kid story, submit it to

www.HeardonthePlayground.com

Your story may be selected for the next edition of *Heard on The Playground*.